"DADDY'S HOME"

"DADDY'S HOME"

A Practical Guide for Maximizing the
Most Important Hours of Your Day

GREG JOHNSON
AND
MIKE YORKEY

Tyndale House Publishers, Inc.
Wheaton, Illinois

Unless otherwise noted, all Scripture quotations are from the Holy Bible,
New International Version. © 1973, 1978, 1984 International Bible Society.
Used by permission of Zondervan Bible Publishers.

Scripture quotations marked NKJV are from the New King James Version
of the Bible, © 1979, 1980, 1982, 1984 by Thomas Nelson, Inc., Nashville,
Tennessee, and are used by permission.

Library of Congress Cataloging-in-Publication Data

Johnson, Greg, date
    Daddy's home : a practical guide for maximizing the most
  important hours of the day / Greg Johnson and Mike Yorkey.
    p. cm.
  Includes index.
  ISBN 0-8423-1093-2
    1. Fathers—Religious life. 2. Fatherhood—United States.
3. Fathers—Time management. 4. Christian life—1960. I. Yorkey,
Mike. II. Title.
BV4529.Y67   1992
248.8'421—dc20   92-12243

97 96 95 94 93 92
8   7   6   5   4   3   2   1

To all of my pastors
who by their lives and words have shaped my
character and been used by God to mold my
life as a Christian, husband, and father:
Louis Brunner, Matt Knighten,
Jan David Hettinga, Kevin Cavanaugh,
Jay Pankratz, and Roc Bottomly.

To those who served
as my official and unofficial mentors,
your friendship and example have meant
more than you'll ever know:
the late Paul Lassen, Dan Brunner, Bart
Brewer, Wayne Cordiero, Sean McCartin,
Tim Johnson, Dave Scherrer, and Tom Hess.

Finally, to my lifetime wife, Elaine,
and our two boys, Troy and Drew,
who each day challenge me to love
as Christ loved the church.

GREG JOHNSON

I dedicate this book to my wife, Nicole,
and our two children, Andrea and Patrick.

To my parents, Pete and Anne Yorkey.

And to Elizabeth Kennedy and
her daughter, McKenzie.

MIKE YORKEY

CONTENTS

"DADDY'S HOME"

"DADDY'S HOME"

CONTENTS

"DADDY'S HOME"

ACKNOWLEDGMENTS

*I*t's customary to thank some people when you write a book.

To our wives, Nicole Yorkey and Elaine Johnson, who stuck with us throughout the researching and writing of this book.

To several people at Focus on the Family: Dr. James Dobson, an extraordinary leader; Rolf Zettersten, the executive vice president who brought us into the ministry; and Dean Merrill, the vice president of periodicals, our boss and mentor.

To Sandra P. Aldrich, the senior editor of *Focus on the Family* magazine, who did a superb job of editing the final manuscript, and to Tom Hess, editor of *Citizen* magazine, for his suggestions.

To Kim Kennedy for her notes of encouragement and prayers on our behalf.

To Bob Newman and Craig Torstenbo for their expert assistance with the Top Ten lists scattered throughout.

To Mark Eaton and Kevin Cavanaugh who went above and beyond during the interview process. Their insights were life changing.

To Mike's next-door neighbors, Dr. Jonathan and Rhonda Weston, who kept us laughing and let us borrow their computer.

To all the fathers who answered the questionnaires and participated in the follow-up interviews, we know who you are, and we greatly appreciate your cooperation.

PREFACE
In The Beginning

*O*ne hundred and sixty-eight hours a week.

That's all the time God gives us every seven days. And like a regular paycheck that has to cover a fortnight of bills, it never stretches far enough. Time is the coin of the realm for today's busy families, and we must spend this precious resource wisely. "For several thousand years, mankind has used money as the primary means of establishing value," says Christian researcher George Barna in *The Frog in the Kettle*. "While money will continue to play a major role in our decisions and actions, by the year 2000 we will have shifted to using *time* as our dominant indicator of value."

Some time choices are already made for us: we have to work, sleep, commute, shop, eat, and do household chores. But we all have some discretionary time, however limited that may be.

We define discretionary time as the hours between when we arrive home from work until we go to bed, plus the weekends. (We are discounting discretionary time on weekday mornings since most fathers are making the mad dash for work.) That's why the early evening hours are the most important hours of the day. What we do during this block of time has a profound effect on our marriage, our children, our physical health, and our spiritual life.

How can you maximize your hours at home? Throughout this book, we'll share anecdotes and insights from our own lives and from one hundred Christian fathers who are getting the job done.

In researching this book, we wrote church pastors around the country and asked, "Who are the best fathers in your congregation?" Then we approached the Focus on the Family Public Affairs staff and asked Lindsay Spaethe and Kurt Leander, who travel and represent the ministry, to give us a list of exceptional fathers they have met on the road.

Our next step was to mail two hundred questionnaires. We received 101 back. The survey questions and results are shared in the first appendix in the back of the book.

From the pool of fathers who completed the questionnaire, we conducted lengthy phone interviews with fifty-two. For confidentiality's sake, we've used fictitious names and cities throughout the book.

One father we talked to seemed well schooled on the American male dilemma: "The nineties guy is really confused about his changing roles. When you compound this with the vacuum of strong male models who pursue Christ and nurture their families, we've got the makings of a real crisis.

"Since we'll never rid our lives of all the weeds we've sown, it seems as though we're moving from one 'out-of-balance' position to another. It's making us ineffective husbands and fathers."

While a small percentage of men are so out of balance they don't know which way is up, most of us have an idea when life is off kilter. The *big* question is: Will we do anything about it?

This book covers a dozen or so foundational areas the men we talked with felt were most important. As you read, you'll probably come across chapters that seem to scratch the surface; they don't answer every question you have on the subject. That was intentional; otherwise *"Daddy's Home"* would be too thick, and you wouldn't read it!

IN THE BEGINNING

What type of man should take a few precious hours (hours he doesn't have) to pull something practical from these pages? Here's who:

- Fathers who are looking for ways to play a greater role in their children's lives.
- Husbands who need some motivation and practical ideas to rekindle their relationship with their brides.
- Men who have trouble balancing husband and father priorities with their spiritual lives.
- Basically, men who want to maximize the most important hours of their day—men like us.

Let us state at the outset, however, that Greg Johnson and Mike Yorkey are not perfect husbands and fathers—nor will we ever be. We know that when we're confronted by our wives, children, and especially God, we're men in need of work. But we're committed to maximizing those most important hours, especially after having written this book!

It doesn't take a media guru to notice that fathering is "in" these days; we live in the "nurturing nineties," we are told. Hollywood and Madison Avenue have stepped into the breach, giving us their image of the thoroughly modern dad. Nurturing fathers are sitcoms' hottest characters, and advertisers are zeroing in on the warmth between a father and child to sell everything from life insurance to razor blades. Folgers coffee commercials show Mom discovering Dad snoring in an easy chair with a sleeping baby in his arms. "The baby was up all night, you've got to make the morning bright," goes the jingle. In a J. C. Penney ad, several dads are pictured taking their kids to the movies, leaving the office with children under their arms, and showing another youngster how to chalk a pool cue.

These rosy pictures of "involved dad," however, are clouded by some dark statistics. We know that 50 percent of America's families eventually divorce, and the effect on children is incalculable. We know that one out of every four children will live with a step-parent before the age of sixteen. We know that if present trends continue, we will soon have more single-parent and step-parent families than traditional families.

If you shrug at these stats, then consider this letter a church pastor received from a third-grade teacher. Keep in mind that this letter was not written by an inner-city teacher but by one living in the Midwest.

> I look at my seventeen students, and I feel a deep sadness. Out of these seventeen, only eight have both natural parents. Two of these watch dirty movies with their parents. One has been sexually abused by her brother.
>
> Sally's mother walked out on her father and the two children when they were babies. When Sally was seven, she witnessed her father's death in an explosion near their home. She and her four-year-old brother live with a relative, who doesn't take the best care of them.
>
> Amy's father was killed shortly after her mother remarried. Rosemary has no idea where her father is.
>
> Peter's mother left town, and her husband has to raise the four boys alone. Peter started stealing last year to get attention. He said he missed his mom.
>
> Barry's mother remarried. He hasn't seen his father in two years because he doesn't pay child support. Barry lives in another world.
>
> Betsy gets to see her father when he comes to visit their home. Her dad's new wife hates Betsy because she looks too much like her mother.
>
> Bill has no idea who his father is. His mother is a lesbian. His grandmother raises him.
>
> Andrea loves both her father and mother. She wants to see them get back together. Her mother works at a tavern at night and takes the children there sometimes.

IN THE BEGINNING

Bruce's mother has had three husbands. All have walked out on her. Little Bruce said his real daddy came back to see him one day. But he was gone two days later. I cried with him.

Last week, two other children had to transfer to another school. It seems that their moms and dads had separated.

You wonder what's going through parents' heads when you read such stories.

Our only hope in this broken world is Jesus Christ. Only He can fix what ails this messed-up society. That's why it was a tremendous encouragement to survey and interview one hundred Christian fathers. With Christ as their foundation, they understand the importance of keeping their eyes on Jesus, loving their wives, nurturing their children, and leading godly lives. And they offer some practical steps to doing exactly that.

IN THE BEGINNING

INTRODUCTION

*O*ne morning, Greg Johnson walked into my office at Focus on the Family with an intriguing idea.

"Mike," he started, "this fathering and husband business is pretty hard work. I've been married over fifteen years now; and the more I'm into it, the harder it gets. I bet a lot of dads out there feel the same way. What would you think of our writing a book for busy dads?

"Nearly every guy I know who has kids and bills is struggling. We could share practical ideas from other fathers who are doing things right. I don't have time to write this book by myself, and I think we would make a good team."

Greg is editor of Focus on the Family's *Breakaway* magazine for teen guys, while I am editor of *Focus on the Family* magazine, the monthly publication representing Dr. James Dobson's ministry to more than 1.7 million families across America. I joined Focus on the Family in 1986; Greg came on board in the fall of 1989.

Shortly after we agreed to do *"Daddy's Home,"* Memorial Day weekend arrived. Although I understand the significance of the holiday, I've never attended a Memorial Day parade or a ceremony honoring our nation's war dead. But on this Memorial Day, I tried something different—I took my kids to a small cemetery.

My children, Andrea and Patrick, were second and first graders at the time, respectively. I often look for things we can do together, no matter how mun-

1

dane. That morning, we jumped into the car with a couple of their neighborhood friends and drove a few blocks. Already, the mid-morning sun was hot, but the tall oak trees in the cemetery offered a respite from the Southern California heat.

We stepped outside the car and began walking amidst the tombstones. "Look," said Andrea, "this one has a flag in the ground."

Around us, several dozen headstones were decorated with fresh flowers and small American flags. "Those flags tell us that the person who died either was killed in a war or used to be in the military," I explained.

"What war, Daddy?" asked Patrick.

"Well, this person died in 1944, so he must have died during World War II."

"Did he shoot anybody?"

"He probably did, but we can't tell for sure. What we do know is that he died for our freedom."

I could tell the kids didn't understand the word *freedom*, but I was able to talk to them naturally about things I had never talked to them about before. As we strolled from tombstone to tombstone, I discussed the shortness of life and the certainty of death. I also explained that when we die we will go to heaven because we believe in Jesus.

The next day at the office, I told Greg about my exciting morning at the cemetery. "That's strange," he said, "because I took *my* kids to a cemetery yesterday, too. It was one of the most memorable things Troy, Drew, and I have ever done. I think I'm going to make it a yearly tradition."

All of a sudden, we felt a lot better about collaborating on *"Daddy's Home."* Greg and I are a lot alike. We're fathers in our mid-thirties with young families, and it seems as though our marriages and spiritual lives are always in need of a tuneup. In fact, in writ-

ing this book together, we've learned a lot about becoming better fathers, husbands, and Christian men
in the nineties.

Please turn the pages and see if you don't agree.

Greg Johnson &
Mike Yorkey

"DADDY'S HOME"

1

TURNING AIRCRAFT CARRIERS AT THIRTY KNOTS

Men and Change

No warship in the world is larger than the USS *Nimitz*, a nuclear-powered aircraft carrier. The *Nimitz* stretches 1,092 feet long and has 4.5 acres of flight deck. Yet this 100,846-ton "flattop" can zip along in excess of thirty knots, and she can travel a million miles on a tank of gas.

But one thing the *Nimitz* can't do is turn on a dime. If a man fell overboard, the ship would need one to two miles before it could even *begin* to execute an 180-degree turn.

Today's families are much like aircraft carriers. We often get headed in one direction—and it's hard to change course. Other times, the storms of life buffet our boat, but we usually ride it out.

Like the *Nimitz'* abundance of technology and hardware, family life is getting more and more complicated as we steam toward the year 2000. Families need constant attention and maintenance these days, but we also need "down time" to recharge our batteries.

All his days his work is pain and grief; even at night his mind does not rest. This too is meaningless.
Ecclesiastes

A faithful man will be richly blessed, but one eager to get rich will not go unpunished.
Proverbs

The captain of the family is the father. At least, that's been God's design all along. A father's duties include loving his wife and children, providing strong leadership, earning a living to support the family, and imparting spiritual values to his kids. And that's just the short list.

Many of the dads we interviewed felt a bit over-whelmed by the tasks before them, and we don't blame them. Some believed the family ship was moving much too fast—too quick even to think about making a U-turn. Others felt locked into a certain course. But another group of fathers saw that their family ship was headed for rocky shores and certain destruction if they didn't change course. Here are a half-dozen snapshots of men who had the foresight to switch directions.

Exploding Television

One Texas father, Elliot, said he spent the first ten years of his marriage devoted to the love of his life—work. Although success came early, and he tasted the trappings of material wealth, Elliot felt empty inside.

"I was working in the insurance business, and my life was totally work. That's all I did, and I was aver-aging sixty hours a week. I know now that God looks at the heart, and my heart wasn't right."

One March evening, Elliot and his wife, Jerri, re-turned home from a church function around 11:00 P.M. in a driving thunderstorm. About midnight, lightning hit an electrical pole outside their home. Like a powder fuse winding its way to the dynamite keg, the charge followed the electric lines into the house and snaked into the family TV. In microsec-onds, the television set exploded into flames.

MEN AND CHANGE

6

Elliot, not quite asleep, smelled smoke coming from the other end of the house.

"I hurried to the den, where I discovered one of the walls was on fire. In the thirty seconds it took to call the fire department, my path to the front door was cut off by flames. I couldn't go out front to where Jerri had taken the kids—the house was almost fully engulfed. I didn't realize it, though; I was in a state of shock. I escaped out the back, but I severely burned my feet from the smoldering carpet. I never felt the burns until I left the house."

By the time Elliot ran around to the front to join his anxious wife (frantic that her husband was still inside the burning home), all they could do was hold each other and watch their house and all their earthly possessions go up in flames.

"That's when I heard an audible voice," says Elliot. " *'I'm trying to get your attention. This is Me intervening, and you need to turn to Me and make a change in the direction you're heading.'* "

Whether or not God burned down his house, Elliot saw this as a wake-up-and-smell-the-coffee call from the Lord. The experience shook him to the soles of his wingtips, and in the weeks following the loss of his house, he made major changes in his life. He renewed his relationship with the Lord, began working fewer hours, and came to the realization that true wealth is in the family. "My advice to other fathers is not to wait until the Lord hits you over the head with a baseball bat."

MEN AND CHANGE

"One Texas father, Elliot, said he spent the first ten years of his marriage devoted to the love of his life—work. . . . Elliot felt empty inside."

Falling off the Ladder

A few years ago, Norman, a school principal in the Southwest, received the promotion he'd always coveted: school superintendent.

The elevation to district superintendent was supposed to be the capstone on Norm's career. Instead, the responsibility overwhelmed him. At forty-four, his realm encompassed five schools, two hundred teachers, and two thousand students. To keep up, Norm worked away from home fourteen hours a day, seven days a week. The highway to success demanded a terrific toll—his family life.

"I knew what I was doing was wrong," recalls Norm, "but I let my pride get in the way. Sure, the job meant more money, more prestige, but I was sacrificing my family."

Within months, Norm became mentally and physically exhausted. The strain on him and the family was too steep, so he resigned. He walked away from a high-paying, prestigious position without having another one lined up.

For nine months, Norm worked construction and picked up some consulting work to make ends meet. "The Lord blessed us tremendously, though," he says. "We had a lot of wants go unmet, but never a lot of needs."

In the meantime, Norm applied for jobs in public education, though he thought he'd ruined his career. Seventeen times he was called in for interviews (having finished in the top three applicants). Seventeen times he was turned down. Then in mid-August, with the start of the new school year just days away, he received the best news in months: an elementary school wanted him to be their new principal. The only problem was that the school was in Phoenix—three hundred miles away.

"When I sat down with my family, I explained that this was the only job the Lord opened to us and that I had no other jobs to interview for. With that, we prayed together. After lifting our needs, we felt that this was what the Lord wanted us to do."

MEN AND CHANGE

Because the job offer arrived too late for the family to move, Norm commuted to work. He left Sunday afternoon at four and returned home at eleven o'clock on Friday night. Within eight months, the long drives finally caught up with him.

"My physical health went downhill," he says. "One day at school, I collapsed and was taken to the hospital. They thought I had suffered a heart attack, but the specialist said I had the healthiest heart of any forty-five-year-old he knew. He felt it was a delayed reaction to all the stress of the previous year."

Norm began a regimen of diet and exercise—and prayer. His break came when political upheaval toppled the school superintendent in his old hometown. Three members of the local school board approached Norm and asked him to apply for a vacant principal's position.

"Once again, I was in the top three, but this time the Lord opened the door, and I got the job. My family is still number one. What I learned is that when you make right decisions about your family, things work out."

Today, Norm's happy with being just a school principal. "I don't have any more desire to be a superintendent. When I was climbing the ladder, I didn't count the cost on the way up. But when I resigned, I was amazed to see how the Lord lifted the load from me. I knew I did the right thing when I resigned."

Like a Sailor on Furlough

"It was the mid-sixties," says Larry, a real estate developer, "and I was extremely authoritative and intimidating with my family. I really didn't know how to show affection to my wife, Jane. I showed I cared by bringing home the bread. At least, that's the way I saw it."

One memorable night, after the kids were in bed, Jane wanted to sit in the living room and talk with Larry. Imagine that—she just wanted to talk. But Larry gave her a cold shoulder the size of Hulk Hogan's. "I told my wife I had office reading to do, so I huffed and left the living room. We had no communication. Zippo."

Finally, after months of inattention, Jane reached the end of her patience. She took the kids, packed up some belongings, and drove to her parents' place in Houston. Meanwhile, Larry acted like a sailor on his first furlough. "I loved it. I was in seventh heaven. The first week she was gone I could work to my heart's content. But things began to change. By Sunday evening, I was wandering through the house. Then I picked up the Bible, something I hadn't done since high school. I'd always believed in God, but I'd never had a personal relationship." Something was stirring in Larry's heart.

"The next morning, while I was shaving, I turned into a babbling idiot. I was flat-out crying. It was a bad scene, but I got back my composure and went to work." During a chance business meeting later that morning, he noticed a *Youth for Christ* magazine on the guy's desk.

"What's that?" he asked.

The answer prompted many more questions from Larry, who listened to the businessman share the gospel. Later that evening Larry confessed his sins and accepted Christ into his life. "I called Jane with the good news, and I asked her to come home," said Larry. "She knew from my voice something was different. I told her that we would be going to church on Sunday. And then she came to know the Lord two weeks later."

"*I was extremely authoritative and intimidating with my family. I really didn't know how to show affection to my wife, Jane. I showed I cared by bringing home the bread. At least, that's the way I saw it.*"

"Is Daddy Here?"

Paul used to be gone for weeks at a time selling commercial insurance. His territory stretched from the Lone Star State all the way to the Florida beaches.

"I learned that you can make all the money in the world, but then you can wake up and discover that your kids don't know you. It used to be a joke around here that when I got home—the kids would run over to the family picture to make sure it was Daddy."

Paul stopped laughing a long time ago. "I finally realized those are years you never get back," he says, so he decided no more road. No more three-week trips. No more weekends away.

"You have to look at life and see where your priorities are set. What are your kids worth compared to what you can earn at work?"

A lot more, Paul decided.

"So What If I Forgot?"

Richard was used to working seventy hours a week in the restaurant business, an industry infamous for making insane time demands on its employees. "I was a workaholic, and up to the point when I became a Christian, my career was all-important. I expected my wife, Kathy, to subordinate everything to that career and the business. If I had to be gone twelve hours a day, seven days a week, I expected her to tolerate that. So what if I forgot her birthday? So what if I forgot I was supposed to do something with the kids? That was her job. I viewed the family-type things as women's work. I wasn't quite that calloused, but almost."

Once he became a Christian, Richard still loved his work, but he knew his priorities needed major ad-

"I learned that you can make all the money in the world, but then you can wake up and discover that your kids don't know you."

justments. "I *had* to change my life and schedule," he says today. "You can't say you love God and your family if you're not willing to spend time with both. If you don't do that, you're only kidding yourself."

"They Called Me an Idiot"

Ronnie, a CPA living in Southern California, knew he was out of balance at times.

Ronnie went through some rough water when he was bounced out of a Big Eight accounting firm. Losing his job was a blow to his ego, but the Lord opened up a way for Ronnie to start his own accounting business. "I've always had this tremendous fear of losing my job," he confessed. "Even though I knew the Lord was taking care of me, I thought I better hold up my end of the bargain, too." Once, before Ronnie struck out on his own, he was setting up a new computer for a company. He was given an impossible deadline, and if he didn't perform—well, let's just say he'd be pounding the pavement in short order. The long hours wore down his health, and Ronnie got sick—a bad strain of chest flu. "I kept driving myself," he remembers. "It got so bad that I had to hold the door jamb to cough." One afternoon, he hacked so hard that he felt as though he had pulled his ribs out of joint.

The next morning, Ronnie had a 7:00 A.M. breakfast meeting, but he was too sick to pull himself out of bed. Ever the trooper, Ronnie said he *had* to go. His wife, Rhonda, pleaded with him to see a doctor. But he refused.

That's when Rhonda did something Ronnie says more wives should do—she gave him an ultimatum. "If you go to this meeting, then you're telling me your job is more important than our marriage and your health. If you go, our relationship will be destroyed."

That speech caused Ronnie to think—just a little. *Gee, she means it*, he thought. *She's never said anything like that before.*

After more soul searching, Ronnie decided his wife was right. He stayed home and went to see the doctor, where he received proper medical care and a tongue lashing. "The doctor told me what a jerk I was to be working while I was deathly ill. Then he popped my ribs back in place. It turned out that during one of my cough attacks I really had torn ligaments and pulled two ribs out of joint. I was put on half-day work, and when I returned to the job, my boss told me what an idiot I was to jeopardize my health. In fact, a lot of people said the same thing. Everyone could see how stupid I was—everyone but me."

Selling Out

Doug owned a semiconductor manufacturing plant in California's Silicon Valley, but when his kids were five and two, he discovered that the company owned him.

"I was the typical executive, putting in twelve- to fourteen-hour days. Long dinner meetings. Weekend conferences. Frankly, I was getting burned out. My kids were growing up without me."

Even more importantly, Doug had become a Christian after his oldest son, Kelly, was born. As he became exposed to parenting ideas from various Sunday school classes and books, Doug's heart changed. "I knew then that the kids needed a dad at home."

What cemented the change was when he saw Kelly swinging a plastic baseball bat and kicking a ball around the back yard. "If I wanted to see the kids grow up, I'd better be around. Kelly was five years old and Little League and soccer were just around the corner. I wanted to take part in those things and have

"Doug owned a semiconductor manufacturing plant in California's Silicon Valley, but when his kids were five and two, he discovered that the company owned him."

those memories. I wanted to share those times with him. That meant making some adjustments."

Boy, did Doug make some changes! He sold his company, then moved his family back to Texas to be near the grandparents, aunts and uncles, and cousins. (Sorry, California, but Doug said he also liked Texas' old-fashioned values.) Then he set up an office at home and started a small manufacturing rep company. "For months, I'd been talking with my wife, Claudia, about selling the company. Of course, she thought it was a great idea. But let's not paint too bright a picture here. I know a lot of guys can't do that—change jobs or sell their business. I was able to sell the company and come away with enough money to restructure my life for a better organized one, if you will. I was lucky—I got a second chance," said Doug.

Now that he's accepted a less-demanding job, Doug's available a lot more, and he can control his hours. "You know, there is a trade-off of money versus time," he says. "I could work more and make more money, but being involved with my family is more important now."

Then Doug said something all fathers should consider: "I don't think there's a job that you couldn't work all the time. There's always more to do than you can get done in a day. Where do you draw the line? It really comes down to priorities."

Can You Read the Road Signs?

Any of these stories sound familiar?

These fathers pursued their professions for a while at the expense of the most important people in their lives. For some, the most important hours of the day were when they were working . . . feeling productive

MEN AND CHANGE

. . . improving their careers . . . and doing what they believe they were supposed to do.

But these men nearly paid a hefty price. Why?

- Greed
- Pride
- Ignorance
- Misplaced priorities

Are You Ripe for a Change?

These men eventually arrived at the same conclusion: the priorities of work and career goals were out of hand. Fortunately, they made changes before it was too late.

What about you?

We all know it's honorable, right, even biblical for a man to work hard to support his family and provide for the future. But at what cost?

This book won't judge your motives if you're a workaholic. But we will challenge the men who are headed toward a heart-wrenching collision with reality. Take this brief quiz and find out if work *has* replaced your loved ones during the most important hours of your day.

1. After work, do you usually hang around the office and chat with the guys before going home? Yes   No

2. Do you take work home and concentrate on it *before* the kids go to bed? Yes   No

3. Do you mind working over sixty hours a week if you can make more money? Yes   No

4. Are you constantly looking for ways to moonlight? Yes   No

5. Do you have trouble clicking off business when you're home? Yes   No

6. Has your wife stopped complaining that you work too much, even though you are away just as much? Yes No

7. Have you stopped reading for pleasure or pursuing hobbies you used to do? Yes No

8. Has it been more than six months since you've shared your faith with someone? Yes No

9. Is spending time with God a drag? Yes No

10. Do you spend free time thinking about work instead of your wife or kids? Yes No

11. Do you ever spend an afternoon doing nothing? Yes No

12. Do you do paperwork with the TV on more than once a week? Yes No

13. Do you make a habit of working during your lunch hour? Yes No

14. Do you often daydream about moving into a bigger and better house? Yes No

15. Do you look for excuses when asked to serve at church? Yes No

16. Do you regularly miss your children's school or sporting events because of work? Yes No

17. Have you quit exercising like you used to? Yes No

If you said yes to five or more of these statements, then it's time to take a hard look at the appointment book and see where you can change your priorities.

Making the Hard Choices

If you do sense that a change is necessary, look before you leap, but leap—quickly! Do two things first:

MEN AND CHANGE

1. Ask Your Wife What She Thinks

Since you may have already talked (or even argued) about the need for change, it's important she have a say-so on anything major.

A few years ago, a seminary graduate was hired to his first associate pastorate. Soon after he arrived, the senior pastor and two assistants resigned. Out of a misguided sense of duty, the young minister stuck it out and did what he could. For three years he worked heroic hours, usually eighty to one hundred hours a week.

Once the church got over the hump, though, he left (finally) to direct a Christian camp. Before he was hired, he was promised the job wouldn't be that stressful. But later, he was asked—and was expected—to take on more "responsibility." That translated into more hours—seventy a week, in fact.

The young pastor sat down with his wife. They agreed he should resign, which he did the following day.

This man now pastors a large church in Oregon. Before he accepted the new assignment, however, he told the elder board he wouldn't work more than fifty hours a week. "I made a commitment to my family when I resigned from the camp," he says. "I wasn't about to make the same mistake again."

Happily, this case turned out to be cut-and-dried, but your choices may be a little more fuzzy. When that happens, it's a good idea to seek a second opinion.

2. Talk to Your Pastor or a Trusted Friend

If you're like most men, you have to be convinced that it's "logical" before you make any wholesale changes. Someone with more experience than you—perhaps a friend who's been down the same path—can help you think through what might lie ahead.

MEN AND CHANGE

"If you're like most men, you have to be convinced that it's 'logical' before you make any wholesale changes."

What If You're Not Sure?

Let's get real. A little stress at work doesn't mean you should quit and move to the mountains to work as a fire spotter. And overtime for a short period of time doesn't necessarily mean you're out of God's will either. Every career has its peaks and valleys. Hopefully, your job will even out so life can stay in relative balance.

But if sixty-hour work weeks roll by for months at a stretch, with no end in sight, it may be time to check the "life priority" barometer to see if a change is in the forecast.

Leaving your job probably won't be necessary, but you'll need to readjust some priorities to get in better balance. That's where this book will come in handy. Our recommendation: As you read through these pages, choose a couple of areas to work on. Though you may be used to being Superman, now's not the time for leaping tall buildings in a single bound. Let's concentrate on small steps instead.

But what if I'm doing okay? *You may be in big trouble!* A real estate developer in Atlanta justified his twelve-hour days like this:

"Though I work a lot of hours, my family doesn't complain. I've learned the secret of getting them on my side. I simply sit down with each of them and explain that the more I work, the better able I am to provide a nice home, food, clothes, a pool, and other things they want to have. After I use this logic, they always nod their heads in agreement."

Sadly, this man's lost his family—and he doesn't even know it! He's traded the most important years of his kids' lives for BMWs and a pool in the back yard. He's convinced his family that they need "the better things in life" more than they need him. And once they've tasted those goodies, it's hard to go back to the farm.

MEN AND CHANGE

Pursuing luxuries—and only being home a couple of hours a day—are sure signs of twisted priorities. Most often, though, this type of justification is a smoke screen to hide insecurities about being a husband and father.

But fear not. Most likely, you're doing just fine. We sincerely hope so, and if that's the case, this book will be preventative medicine for you—a booster shot of confidence for getting the most out of the precious few hours we have with the ones we love.

Man to Man

1. How many evenings a week do you arrive home from work too late to spend at least an hour with your children and an hour with your wife?

2. What do your weekends look like? Do weekend activities connect you with your family or separate you from them?

3. When you imagine a less-pressured home life, what comes to mind?

MEN AND CHANGE

FATHER KNOWS STRESS

Men at Work

You're sitting in a window seat waiting out another of O'Hare's interminable delays. You've read the complimentary newspaper and the in-flight magazine—even the Boeing 737 safety card! You're bored. So you break a long-held habit: You start a conversation with the businessman sitting next to you.

Before the jet finishes taxiing, it's even money that one of you will pop this question: So, what do you do for a living?

It's a time-honored inquiry dating back to the days of Fred Flintstone. We ask that question so we can quickly size up our new acquaintance—and with the secret hope that he'll ask us what we do.

Why? Well, we are what we do, right?

For most of us, much of our self-esteem and self-worth is tied up in our work. If we're successful in the workplace, we welcome the chance to let the world know. On the flip side, nothing is more debilitating than being fired or laid off. Our sense of purpose—and our ego—is deflated.

That's because work is *very* important to us, as it is to God. Let's not forget that He established people on

I amassed silver and gold for myself, and the treasure of kings and provinces.

I denied myself nothing my eyes desired; . . . My heart took delight in all my work, and this was the reward for all my labor.

Yet when I surveyed all that my hands had done and what I had toiled to achieve, everything was meaningless.

Ecclesiastes

earth to work: "The LORD God took the man and put him in the Garden of Eden to work it and take care of it" (Genesis 2:15). Notice that Adam wasn't given a chaise lounge and directions to the nearest pool.

Nor was Adam told that earning a living was going to be a breeze. These two gems from Proverbs sum up God's feelings: "Lazy hands make a man poor, but diligent hands bring wealth" (10:4); and "The plans of the diligent lead to profit as surely as haste leads to poverty" (21:5).

These points aren't lost on many Christian fathers. "We *have* to work for a living," says one salesman who puts in long hours. "We still have to build a future for our family."

While some fathers choose to work too much, others are being asked—even ordered—to work overtime. In the June 1991 issue of *Focus on the Family*, we printed a timely article, "Jobs vs. Family: Striking a Balance." Author Brian Knowles described the problem for many white-collar workers: "Because of the erosion in our manufacturing base, firms are being forced to offer intangibles, such as a higher quality of service, in order to compete in the world market. This means more and more companies are demanding twelve-hour days and six-day weeks from their employees."

With the economy floundering in the nineties, companies are being driven to the wall. Corporations are "downsizing" their operations—a euphemism for lay-offs—and requiring the remaining employees to manage the same workload.

Sound familiar? If you're in that bind, then you have our sympathy. You're working for a company that believes employees must sacrifice family on the altar of work. Sooner or later, you'll have to decide whether to continue in that anti-family environment. Yes, your career is important, but no job is worth offering up your wife and children.

> *"Work is very important to us, as it is to God. Let's not forget that He established people on earth to work."*

MEN AT WORK

22

If you're contemplating changing jobs, take it to God first. Ask Him for direction, what avenues you should pursue. Then have a friendly chat with your boss. Let him or her know how you feel. Can you do some work at home? Could you get more help? What can be done to reduce the overtime?

Feeling the Squeeze

The fathers we surveyed said they work an average of 51.2 hours a week—ten-hour days, for the most part. That's below the national average of fifty-six hours, but it's still a hefty load. While most of our fathers believed they weren't being overworked, nearly all of them said they felt the squeeze to include family time in the weekdays.

But don't expect corporate America to recognize how much fathers are needed at home. The employee's family life isn't part of the annual report, nor can it be measured on the bottom line. But it should be. The *Wall Street Journal* reported in July 1991 that more than 60 percent of respondents from Fortune 500 corporations said their jobs robbed them of adequate energy and time to do things with their families. What many CEOs don't understand is that work and family are intertwined; if Dad isn't overworked, and his family life is in balance, he will be a happier, more productive employee.

"Don't expect corporate America to recognize how much fathers are needed at home."

Restoring the Balance

Those who had their work lives in balance were quick to share some tips on how they did it. If you're chalking up a lot of overtime, then here are ways you can jog loose a few more hours at home.

The Most Important Hours

Understand what the most important hours of the day are. Okay, what are they? Answer: when you're home, Dad. Or more specifically, the time period between 5:00 and 10:00 P.M.—that stretch when the family can regroup, eat dinner, share their day, and talk about the future.

If you're closing that window of opportunity because you're booking extra hours or crawling along some expressway, then it's hard to perform your fatherly duties.

"The most important hours of the day are . . . when you're home, Dad."

Working Smarter

Have you ever noticed that some people just don't work that well? They're the type who putz around doing a little of this and a little of that and then erupt into a major panic when crunchtime arrives.

Maybe you, too, can work smarter. What's your body clock? Are you a morning person? Or do you do your best work at night? If you get more done in the morning, perhaps you should begin working earlier in the day (if your company has flextime). That way you can get off earlier—and beat the traffic home, thus saving even more time.

I (Mike) do most of my creative work—writing and editing—in the morning because that's when I feel most productive. (In fact, most of my colleagues feel the same way. Memos have been circulated around the department asking that 9:00–11:00 A.M. be distraction free.) When the post-lunch doldrums arrive ("siesta time!"), I turn my attention to less taxing tasks, such as answering my mail and returning phone calls.

Those Restaurant Lunches

Skip going out to lunch. I've seen more time wasted by employees who eat out during lunchtime. Yes, it's

MEN AT WORK

24

nice to be served a prepared meal, but by the time you're seated and given a menu, order an entree, wait for the food to arrive, eat, ask for the check, make the payment—well, say *sayonara* to a huge chunk of time. And that doesn't include the minutes lost driving or walking to the restaurant. (It's a different matter if your job description includes business lunches. Hopefully, your boss considers those events part of your eight- or nine-hour day.)

But if you're working past six or seven o'clock because you and some friends lingered over lunch, then that's not good time stewardship. (It's also not the greatest stewardship of your finances. The tab for eating out can easily cost twenty-five to forty dollars a week.)

Brown-bagging is cheaper and faster—and healthier. If you need a change of scenery during the noon hour, take your lunch to a nearby park or company picnic area.

You also should consider taking a thirty-minute lunch. My father, who worked in the construction trade, always had a half-hour for lunch. That meant his work day ended at 4:30, which gave him time to coach my Little League team.

Setting Priorities

If possible, set your priorities—family or career—early in your marriage. Robert always believed raising a family was more important than his career. Sure, he wanted to excel at his profession, but he made his decision not to pursue the fast track *before* the children came along. "The worst time to choose between family and your job is when you're thirty years old and have a couple of kids," he said. "When your circumstances have been positioned toward upward mobility, it's tough to put on the brakes. I've seen men who didn't want to let the company down, so they put their family second."

Promotion?

Think through any promotion. Does it mean more hours? Will it lead to more travel? Is the money worth it?

What would you do if your boss offered you a raise—albeit modest—but said you might have to put in eight hours of overtime each week? Would you take it? You should role-play this scenario with your wife. Have her take the role of the boss (she'll love that!) offering you a promotion. Perhaps the promotion means ten days of out-of-town travel each month. What would you say?

Living Near Work or Relocating

Live closer to work, or consider relocating to a smaller city. That suggestion is more easily said than done, isn't it? For openers, it's hard to sell a house in today's tough economic climate, and some of us don't want to live in neighborhoods close to work. Or we like where we live. The kids are established in school, and we're active members of the local church.

But living closer to work can be a huge benefit, especially if you're burning up the miles in ninety-minute commutes. By cutting your drive time to a manageable ten or fifteen minutes, you can gain another hour or two a day. That's often enough time to see your daughter's soccer game or coach your son's baseball team. You can retrieve up to ten hours a week. Think about how many family or ministry activities you can do with that extra day!

Sometimes relocating to a smaller city can take the edge off a hectic lifestyle. At thirty-five, Rodney, a graphics designer at UCLA, was gone eleven to twelve hours a day working and slugging it out on the L.A. freeways.

"I hit a midlife crisis," he says. "Not job stress, just life stress. It was a time when God was dealing

MEN AT WORK

with me about what was really important. With a new
baby at home and a wife who felt trapped, we made
the decision to move to the slower pace of Vancou-
ver, Washington. Though I didn't have a job, I knew
a drastic change was needed. God came through and
has provided enough freelance work for us to live on,
plus I get to work at home."

You should realize that moving to a new job—or
city—is a long-range project. It might take a couple
of years to make it happen. But you need to start
thinking about it now.

Dinnertime Break

If you've got to work overtime, take a break during
dinnertime. If you have to work on that sales presenta-
tion, can you do it at home after dinner? Can you catch
up on your business reading after the kids are in bed?

Raymond, who makes his living in sales, quits
what he's doing at five o'clock and heads home. "I'm
getting better at it," he says. "I've gotten it down to
the point where I'm with the family for dinner, and I
have time to spend with the kids before putting them
to bed. I don't resume my sales calls until they're
asleep.

"Unfortunately, long hours come with my job.
That's a negative. In my line of work, the more I
work, the more I make. I've got to learn to shut the
door. I've got to be the one who says enough is
enough."

Switching Off the Business Mode

When you are home, switch off the business mode. I
(Mike) am sometimes in a fog when I arrive home.
I'm still thinking about the story I was editing or an
upcoming deadline. But I'm learning to snap out of it.
I remind myself that I have to *actively* listen to my
wife as she tells me about her day.

MEN AT WORK

*"If you've got to
work overtime,
take a break
during
dinnertime."*

27

When Rick, a New England father, arrives home, his wife acts as a buffer between him and the kids for the first fifteen minutes. They'll catch up on each other's day in their bedroom while he changes clothes. Once he's measured the family temperature, he's geared up for whatever the evening holds.

Other men we talked with pray in the car on the way home. By switching off the radio and clearing out the day's stresses, they're able to allow the Lord to prepare them. If your wife's been home with small kids all day (or at work herself), you'll probably be "on duty" no matter what type of day you had. You can either resent it or deal with it by calling on God's power to help you handle whatever happens.

Maximizing Hours at Home

Make the most of the hours you are home. Quality family time doesn't bite you on the leg when you walk through the front door. You've got to be creative and look for things to do together. You can walk your kids to a park, organize a bike ride, or take them for a swim at the municipal pool. Sometimes kids will balk at doing something with Dad because they don't want to leave their friends. Invite the friends along too.

Play catch, hit tennis balls, shoot baskets. One of the best investments you can make is to mount a basketball rim over the driveway. "It's essential to be involved in what the kids are interested in," said Andy. "With my dad, he was always at the office and not with us. That's why for a number of years I've been a basketball coach for third- and fourth-graders. All three of my boys went through the program, and now they're helping out as referees. I would say that's the most important thing we did together."

And one last tip: take advantage of daylight savings time. When the days are long and the evenings are warm, you can do many outdoor activities.

MEN AT WORK

Don't let the sun go down without doing something together.

Your Wife's Work

Ask yourself whether your wife should be employed outside the home. A working mom (*all* moms are working moms, but we're referring to moms employed outside the home) has it really tough. After putting in an eight- or nine-hour day, she returns home for the "second shift." It's a recipe for marital stress, we believe, and if it's at all possible, the mom should stay home. The kids need her, plain and simple. The popular culture would have you believe that both parents are working these days. But that's not necessarily true. According to U.S. Department of Labor statistics, 41.3 percent of all married mothers with preschool children are full-time homemakers. Another 20 percent work part time, some only a few hours a week. You add these two figures up, and that means 61 percent of all mothers with preschool children are spending most of their time raising their kids.

In our survey, only one-third of our fathers said their wives work outside the home, but many of those mothers work part time. In addition, the *Washington Post* reported statistics from the Department of Labor showing that mothers entering the work force declined in 1990—the first such decline in four decades! "The numbers are still small, but we are seeing more and more women saying it's not worth trying to be a mother *and* hold down a full-time job," said Ellen Galinsky, co-president of the research-oriented Families and Work Institute and a widely regarded expert on women and work.

Of course, we recognize that exceptions exist, and there are families in which the mother *must* work. Some areas of the country—especially the major cities on each coast—have stratospheric housing costs, and

MEN AT WORK

"Make the most of the hours you are home. Quality family time doesn't bite you on the leg when you walk through the front door."

it's all a family can do to make the monthly house payment.

A mortgage lender recently explained this phenomenon to me (Mike): "As housing costs went through the roof in the 1970s and 1980s, fathers responded by working longer hours and taking second jobs. When inflation and housing prices continued to soar, families sent the mother back into the work force. When that wasn't enough, banks relaxed their lending policies with 90 percent loans and low adjustable "start" rates in order to qualify more families. Now that we're in the 1990s, we've seen real estate values across the country flatten out or actually depreciate. That's because there's very little families can do to increase income these days."

George Will, in a 1991 *Newsweek* column, said Americans' real after-tax incomes have risen a barely perceptible 0.5 percent since 1973. The nearly twenty years of income stagnation is unprecedented since the start of the Industrial Revolution.

"As many workers' real incomes have declined, families have maintained living standards by sending more mothers into the work force, with consequent family stresses and a pervasive erosion of the sense of well-being," wrote Will.

Should your wife work outside the home? That's a tough call. The question should always be prayerfully considered. If the kids are old enough, their input could be valuable, too. Explain to them that a stay-at-home mom means no trips to Disney World, but Mom can take the kids to local museums and city pools.

Some men are adamant about the importance of Mom's being there for the kids. "I'm a blue-collar worker," said Pete, who makes less than twenty-five thousand dollars a year. "I believe my wife should stay home. It's a real conviction with me. We've got to do what's important."

MEN AT WORK

30

Pete, who has six children, says there are plenty of days when he ignores the neighborhood ice cream truck. "But we are never lacking," he says. "We may think we're suffering, but in Africa, we'd be millionaires."

Weekends

Reserve the weekends for the family. If you let work—the Monday-through-Friday variety—encroach on your weekends, you're headed for misery. Christopher, a salesman for a marketing firm, still puts in

What Does It Really Cost To Send Mom Back Into the Work Force?

BEFORE MOM TAKES THAT JOB, consider the cost. Start by deducting payroll taxes, child-care expenses, new clothes, maintaining a second car, and meals away from home (that includes restaurant lunches and take-out since Mom is usually too wiped out to cook dinner). Once you subtract those expenses, Mom will probably net just a couple of hundred dollars a month, if that.

Then consider the intangibles. Sure, stay-at-home moms are pooped out by the end of the day, but moms employed outside the home are even more frazzled. There will be less time to serve at church, less energy to pursue a relationship with God, less personal time, and less motivation for romance. Disciplining and loving the children will get pushed aside from tiredness. "Fatigue makes cowards of us all," Green Bay Packer coach Vince Lombardi once said.

Could your wife earn the same amount by working on a side business at home? Look for novel ways to bring in extra income. Could she start an at-home business or work part time a couple of days a week? Twenty-six million people—10 percent of the U.S. population—now work at least part time in their home. Many of them are women who jumped off the career track to become mothers and raise a family. Nine percent of our surveyed fathers said their wives had home-based businesses.

One of the most successful articles in *Focus on the Family* magazine in 1991 was "Ways for Moms to Make Money at Home" by Cheri Fuller. She did an excellent job of describing the benefits and pitfalls of starting a home business. Without a doubt, home businesses are a growth industry.

For instance, our family (the Yorkeys) has a side business. We operate a little tennis racket stringing shop out of our home, which allows Nicole to string rackets during the day. We also string at night after the kids are in bed. The couple of hundred bucks it brings in each month is a real boost to the family finances.

fifty- and sixty-hour weeks, but he's stopped working on weekends.

"Saturday and Sunday are for the kids," says Christopher. "They should know that from Friday night to Sunday is family time and that we're going to do something together, whether it's playing baseball, going to Sea World, or whatever."

Tim, a family physician, says he keeps his weekends free for family activities by not seeing patients on Wednesdays. "I take a day off in the middle of the week to run errands and catch up on my paperwork. Sometimes, I'll volunteer a morning at the local indigent health-care facility. Since I've tied up loose ends on Wednesday, these things are not on my mind Saturday or Sunday."

Tim understands that's one of the luxuries of being self-employed in medicine—calling his own shots. "You have to avoid the temptation to fill up every weekday with scheduled appointments," he says.

Tim also tries to keep Sunday as the Sabbath, a time for family worship and family time together. To do that, they plan ahead so that when friends ask them to do something on Sunday, they already have an answer prepared.

Taking Stock

If you are out of balance, take stock and make changes. "I have been out of balance for periods of time," says Antonio, a manufacturer's representative in Southern California. "It took a lot of energy to start our new business, and occasionally the stress of things good or bad could throw it out of balance."

One day, Antonio sat down and made a list. On one sheet, he wrote down what was important in life. On another sheet, he wrote what wasn't important. During a time of reflection, Antonio realized he had to restrict his after-hour business. "Time management is an important thing with families. I've had to learn to say no. Now I've made a commitment to make sure my time matches up with my priorities, and it's really helped keep me in balance."

Another father, Skip, says, "We set priorities in business life, so there's no reason we shouldn't do that with our families as well. We need to understand which way God wants us to set our priorities." During the week, Skip tries to participate in his children's activities, although some events, such as a Cub Scout field trip starting at 3:00 P.M., are impossible to make.

Another father, Timothy, totally revamped his priorities simply after looking at the family photo album. "I decided children just grow up too fast for me to invest my time in selling another piece of commercial property. Today, I make a conscious effort to maintain a balance between work and home."

"If you are out of balance, take stock and make changes."

33

Faith

Believe God's promises. Gregory used to work eleven and twelve hours a day, but after five years of his burning the family candle at both ends, his marriage fell apart. When he became a Christian a while later, Gregory remarried. Inside, he felt different about his reasons for working so much.

"I first read God's promises; then I really started to believe them, especially the one where it says that God will provide for all your needs. I thought, *Okay, Lord, I'll slow down and trust You to bring in enough work so the business can survive.* These days, I won't work more than ten hours a day. I'm not always able to get what I want, but we always have what we need."

A Family Mission Statement

Make a family mission statement. Many companies operate from a brief mission statement, a quick-hitting document that outlines the company's goals and vision for the future. It's an effective way to keep a company on course.

Write a family mission statement with your wife. It should be concise and to the point. Then post it in a conspicuous place where all the family members can see it.

Combining Priorities

If overtime or long hours are unavoidable, combine priorities. Many men must work a fifty- or sixty-hour week to keep the wife home and the family adequately provided for. Julius compensates for his fifty-five-hour week by volunteering with four- and five-year-olds at the church, the class his own kids are in. That way, Julius gets to spend another couple of hours with his children each week.

MEN AT WORK

34

Planning Your Week

Plan your week. Don takes a lot of ribbing from friends for a beginning-of-the-week ritual he initiated years ago. From the beginning of their marriage, Don and his wife, Rhonda, have gone out for a piece of pie and a cup of coffee every Sunday night. Shortly after the waitress clears the apple pie à la mode plates from the table, Don and his wife reach for their personal calendars. For the next hour, they go over their schedules—work, church activities, and kid's programs—for the coming week.

"Several friends have made fun of us, but those calendars eliminate surprises and give us a chance to plan," says Don, who works in medical sales. Occasionally his work takes him out of town on short business trips. These overnight absences are noted on the calendars. "This process saves a lot of grief and conflict," says Don.

You and Your Desk

Know that you're not married to your desk. Although it's been said a million times, it bears repeating one more time. No one who reaches the end of life has ever looked back and said, "Oh, I wish I had spent more time at the office instead of with my kids." We only go through this season of fathering one time, so let's make the most of it.

Our guess is that if you've read this far with us, then you really have a desire to be a good husband and father. Sadly, however, many fathers grew up with dads who were poor examples of what a Christian father should be.

Larry Crabb, the noted family counselor and author of several books, conducted a seminar in Colorado Springs where he asked 350 men if their own dads were good role models. Only *thirty* men raised their hands!

MEN AT WORK

"No one who reaches the end of life has ever looked back and said, 'Oh, I wish I had spent more time at the office instead of with my kids.' "

What was your father like? Our next chapter addresses this question.

Man to Man

1. Why is your work important to you—ego, sense of duty, financial concerns, love of the work itself, family's expectations? Rank your responses from most to least important.
2. List and prioritize suggestions in this chapter that look "do-able" for you.
3. Can you think of other ways that you can reserve more time for your family?

MEN AT WORK

THE ACORN DOESN'T FALL TOO FAR FROM THE TREE

Men and Their Dads

N*ot* long after I (Mike) married Nicole, we moved to her native Switzerland so I could learn a little French and a *lot* about her Swiss culture. We were footloose—as much as you can be in the Old Country—and fancy free without children. Nicole worked as a trilingual secretary while I gave tennis lessons and strung rackets.

After a year in Switzerland, we decided, well, if Nicole becomes pregnant, so be it. Not that we were *ready* for children, but we were open to the idea of having kids. We felt it was time. But nothing happened on the fertility front for six months or so. In the meantime, we decided to move back to California so I could begin my career in journalism. Before we left Switzerland, however, my parents flew over to Zurich and joined us on a month-long jaunt through France and Italy.

Children's children are a crown to the aged, and parents are the pride of their children.
Proverbs

Surely I have been a sinner from birth, sinful from the time my mother conceived me.
Psalms

On the Trans-European Express train from Rome to Florence, Nicole said she felt different. "I feel like a mother," she said. "I think I'm pregnant."

"Oh, really?" I said, popping my head out of a Robert Ludlum novel. The Italian countryside was passing by in a blur—and my mind was traveling a hundred miles an hour, too.

In Florence, Nicole went to a *pharmacia* and bought one of those pregnancy test kits. Back in our hotel room, she shook the test tube and peered at the contents. There was no ring in her urine.

"But I *know* I'm pregnant," she shrieked.

"That's not what the test says," I replied.

"Well, I'm buying a Swiss test next time."

A week later, at the Hotel de Lutece in Paris, Nicole took a Swiss-made pregnancy test out of the box. Within minutes, the results confirmed what Nicole already knew: we were to become parents in about eight months.

Time out, I thought. *I'm going to become a father? But I don't know what to do!*

I felt uneasy the rest of our trip, and I think it was because I was entering fatherhood without the foggiest idea of what I was supposed to do. That little bundle of joy wouldn't arrive with an owner's manual.

The fathers we interviewed agreed. "Of all the things you do that are important, fathering is something you don't have *any* training at all in," one dad told me during an interview. "I took a lot of courses in college to learn my profession, but I didn't learn a thing on becoming a good father."

Sure, we can read books, talk to friends, and view one of Dr. Dobson's film series, but the way we parent is often the way our fathers parented us. *The acorn doesn't fall too far from the tree.* "You know," says one father, "the lyrics of a country song go like this: 'I'm getting more and more like my father every day.' That song kind of hits home with me." Another dad added,

"You take what you can from your father. And it certainly helps if your father was a good role model, a willing leader, and a spiritual teacher." Some men have watched themselves become more like their fathers as they grew older—and they didn't always like it. "Unfortunately, I've repeated a lot of the things I disliked in my father," says Randall, a truck driver.

As for me (Mike), my father was always there, and twenty-five years later I can still remember practicing baseball pitching with him after dinner. But for all he did, I've struggled to be the father I ought to be.

Why is it that many of us don't feel properly equipped to be good fathers? Why are we groping in the dark?

The reason is that many of us grew up in homes where the father was not a good example—or he wasn't there at all. Divorce has became an epidemic over the past three decades, and many of today's crop of fathers are still trying to get their parenting feet underneath them.

Work First, Emotions Second

"Did I have a good role model as a father? No, not really," confessed Bruce. "He worked all the time. He didn't spend a lot of time with the family. My father was a product of the Depression, and he grew up feeling as though he had to work all the time."

Many of our fathers were raised in an era when it was "unmanly" for a father to say "I love you" to his kids. One fellow told me that his father never expressed his love. "To this day, he's never told me," he said, and it still sticks in his craw.

A. J. Foyt, the four-time winner of the Indianapolis 500, had a father who couldn't bring himself to say how proud he was of his son's accomplishments. Nor

MEN AND THEIR DADS

"Of all the things you do that are important, fathering is something you don't have any training at all in."

could he tell his son that he loved him, according to a feature story in *Sports Illustrated*.

Tony Foyt was a top midget car driver, who later became one of A. J.'s mechanics. They were a team, working side by side in Gasoline Alley. But Tony's praise was sparse, and he couldn't bring himself to utter those three simple words.

Just before Tony died in 1983, A. J. and the family were at his bedside. The doctor said, "If you have anything to say to each other, or if you're holding back, you ought to say it. I'll wait outside."

When the doctor left, A. J. could barely speak.

"Well, Daddy, things aren't working out like we hoped."

"I know it," said Tony.

"You have anything you want to talk about?"

"No, not really."

"Well, I don't really have much to say. If anything ever happens, I'll do what I can to try to carry on."

"I know that," Tony said. "But don't worry about things."

"Are you *sure* you ain't got something to tell me?"

"No," replied the dying father. "I've told you everything."

Good Role Models

Todd, a successful building contractor, never took his eyes off his father when he was growing up. "We never caught him lying or being hypocritical," he says. "He also trusted us and gave us a lot of responsibility. Even when we royally screwed up, he never stepped in and dictated to us what we should do. For instance, if we wanted to buy something, and he knew it was totally worthless, he'd tell us what he thought, but then he'd let us buy it anyway. And you know what? He was always right."

Another father, Neils, also grew up with a father who was an excellent role model. "When you look back twenty, thirty years, you remember certain things about your parents. I recall going to the public tennis courts in Miami with my mom and dad. I must have been ten years old at the time, and when one of the courts opened up, my parents insisted that my brother and I play each other first. They sat on the bench and watched us play.

"I like to think they were making a sacrifice for us, but looking back, I think they got more joy from watching us play than they would have gotten from playing themselves."

Neils' father never belittled his son's dreams. If his son announced that he wanted to become a Baltimore Oriole ballplayer, then it was time to play catch in the back yard, "as if the major-league scouts were right there," he said.

As he grew up, Neils' dreams changed—but not his father's encouragement. Neils wanted to become a doctor, and his first step was his acceptance into the pre-med program at Duke University. The out-of-state tuition fees were hefty, but that never daunted Neils' father, who worked as a sales clerk at the local Sears.

"My dad was the sole provider for the family, and his Sears salary was lower middle class," remembers Neils. "But that never mattered. One semester, he told me they were running a little short on money. When I got home that summer, the living room was depleted of furniture. My mother said something about redecorating the place, but I knew the furniture was sold off to pay for my tuition."

Some of us, however, didn't have heroic fathers. One man we interviewed, Richard, was raised in a home without a dad.

MEN AND THEIR DADS

"Many of our fathers were raised in an era when it was 'unmanly' for a father to say 'I love you' to his kids."

When Richard was three, his father divorced his mother and split for a better life in California. But three years later his dad died when he was struck by a car. Richard's mother was never the "motherly type," he says, so he was put in an orphanage shortly after his father's death.

"The Lord had His hand on me because I believe in what the Bible says about His taking care of widows and orphans," says Richard. "When I was growing up, I always thought I would grow up and be a dynamite dad when my turn came around."

What spurred Richard was ghastly childhood memories. He remembers what it was like living in a dormitory with forty other kids when he was six years old. He can remember waking up one night crying because a rat was chewing on his thumb. No one ever heard his cries, and to this day, he still has a scar on his thumb—and his heart.

In junior high, Richard bused tables in a cafeteria-type restaurant alongside another young teen, Hank. The two became fast friends, and before long, Richard moved in with Hank's family. One of Richard's managers in the restaurant took a liking to the two boys, and he invited them over to his home on Friday nights to talk shop. "I remember picking his brain about business until long after midnight," says Richard.

Later, Richard and Hank became business partners, and they opened a fried chicken restaurant in Texas. Over a period of ten years, they built more restaurants throughout the Southwest. Then, several years ago, the pair sold the chain to a West Coast firm. Today, Richard and Hank are semi-retired and living next door to each other on an eighty-acre spread in rural Texas!

"When Richard came to live at our house, we both didn't have a dad—my parents were divorced," says Hank. "One thing that has been important to us, since we both came from broken homes, was that we

MEN AND THEIR DADS

decided early on we were going to marry once, for life, and we were going to try to be good fathers to our children."

Not that fathering has been without its difficulties for Richard, who confesses to making a few mistakes along the way. "One of my problems is that I've been too serious," he says. "I have to force myself to play with the kids. Usually, when I'm with them, I'm still trying to teach. On a recent trip to Hawaii, I tried to tell the kids how much it costs to fly halfway across the Pacific so they'd appreciate it. I thank the Lord that we had the money to go, but I think I overdid it."

A Mentor Arrives

Isn't it amazing how these young boys—growing up without fathers—had such a deep desire to make it right when their turn came around? Their commitment shows that all things are possible through Christ.

Arthur, a pharmacist in South Carolina, saw his father divorce his mother and pack up and leave home shortly after Arthur's eighth birthday. The pain of a missing father intensified when he was a teenager. Dad wasn't home to play catch and run pass routes with or cheer him on at track meets. "A void was there," says Arthur, who still feels the pain today.

The Lord brought a role model to Arthur, a brother-in-law who was nearly ten years older than he. "Bob was my stand-in father who encouraged me, especially when it came time to go out for the track and football teams. I was hesitant; I felt insecure. But Bob helped me and was a good companion."

The Lord also brought a mentor to Richard, the orphan who started a restaurant chain in Texas. Richard's special person was Granny, a woman in her sixties who rented a room to the nineteen-year-old boy. "I lived with Granny as a boarder for ten years, and she taught me a lot about life. She was a neat woman with a great deal of wisdom. I never had grandparents that I knew, but I've always loved older people because they've been down the long, dusty roads. They have words of wisdom to pass along."

Fortunately, or sometimes unfortunately, we become the same type of father our dads were to us. This repetition also affects how well we maximize those most important hours at home. Though it's beyond the scope of this book to deal with deep-seated hurts, we talked to a lot of men who were certain their fathers affected their ability to be a good dad.

Affected, but didn't control.

In the late sixties, my dad (Greg) decided to do his own thing—without the family. He sold a little real estate, but when the market went bad, he chose alcohol and gambling as his occupations. It wasn't long before the family began to disintegrate. Life dealt us a lousy hand: Mom didn't have much of a husband, and my brother, my sister, and I didn't have much of a dad.

Then one day Dad came home and told Mom he wanted a divorce. I was thirteen at the time—and devastated. We were forced to move from a secure home to an ant-infested duplex while Dad went to start another life with another wife. Mom was forced to go to work, and we kids tried to piece our lives back together.

For a young teen trying to survive adolescence, life without Dad didn't seem all that fair. Meanwhile, Dad's second marriage busted after a few months, and he turned to the bottle more than before. When Mom remarried, she moved away with her new husband. Since it was my senior year, I didn't want to leave Eugene, Oregon, so I moved in with Dad and his new girlfriend. He wasn't the world's greatest role model, but we sure had fun together. Dad was cool, I thought, because we'd occasionally smoke dope together. (Did I mention we weren't churchgoers?)

After I graduated from high school, I thought I'd better try the college route. My life had absolutely no direction. At my lowest point, however, the Lord led my high school sweetheart, Elaine, to explain in fuller detail what it meant to be a Christian. She convinced me that Jesus was real. After I turned my life over to Him, my attitudes on certain behaviors changed, too. I was a new creation, and I grew rapidly in my faith. When Elaine and I married a couple of years later, we had Christ in our marriage. So I suffered no ill-effects from my father's example, right?

Well . . . not exactly. While every single sin of my father wasn't passed down to the next generation (that's me!), I'm still—nearly twenty years later—dealing with the consequences of my past actions. I'm certain it will be a never-ending battle for the rest of my life.

Though Dad's no longer on this earth, I have never stopped loving him. For all of his bad traits, he had many good ones as well. Along with a ton of little stuff, he taught me to be concerned for my friends and not to be a cheapskate when it comes to making memories. But let's face it. Dad wasn't able to teach me anything about being the father the Lord wants me to be. Here's what I've tried to do to make up for that loss:

1. *I've gathered all the good information on fatherhood I could.* Mike was right a few pages back when he mentioned the value of books and videos. They've served as an invaluable resource to me.

2. *I'm constantly looking for unofficial fathering mentors.* Fortunately, mentors haven't been too hard to find at Youth for Christ and Focus

MEN AND THEIR DADS

"Fortunately, or sometimes unfortunately, we become the same type of father our dads were to us."

on the Family. During my work day, I've learned a lot from my colleagues. One father told me, "When I see someone doing a good job, I try to find out his secret." That's what I'm doing all the time.

3. *I've learned that I have to be totally committed to the marriage.* Divorce is not an option for Elaine or me. Any problem can be dealt with where Christ is present. While we've faced our share of struggles and would consider counseling should the need arrive, so far our faith and commitment have steered us through.

Looking Ahead

Did you have a father who was a poor role model? If you did, that doesn't mean you're doomed to be a deadbeat dad. Only you can determine whether your past will affect you negatively. If it does, then you should invest in a few sessions with a recommended counselor. You can overcome ingrained problem areas—but it'll be hard work. The result, however, will be worth the effort. Don't settle for second best.

Now that we're older, we realize how quickly our days of youth passed. If you felt cheated in some way, you don't have to pass on to your kids the mistakes you had to endure. You can commit yourself to starting a new branch of the family tree. If you were fortunate enough to come from a good home, write down all the positive things your dad did. Most likely, your notebook will be filled with the little things you did together. Add these things to your family life.

In the next chapter, we'll give you a few ideas on activities you can do with your family.

MEN AND THEIR DADS

Man to Man

1. What were your greatest concerns when you first learned that you were going to be a father?

2. In what ways are your style and actions as a father influenced by the personality and behavior of your own father or of another mentor?

3. What good role modeling are you offering to your children right now? What changes in role modeling would you like to achieve?

MEN AND THEIR DADS

4

FOUR WORDS YOU'LL NEVER WANT TO SAY

Men and Their Kids

Many of the fifty interviews Mike and I conducted were memorable, but for me, one affected me above all the others.

I was talking with a professional man about his job, one with a lot of out-of-state travel. "The first ten to twelve years after the kids were born, my work took me away quite a bit," Roy began. "My wife was really good about it, and she did a great job of raising our three kids. When they hit early adolescence, however, it suddenly dawned on me that I had missed out on a great deal. After much reflection, I did something I never thought I could do: I quit that high-paying job. Then I went out and found a new job that would keep me close to home. But despite all I did, it was too late," says Roy.

"No matter how hard I tried to put myself back into my kids' lives, it didn't work. They had adjusted to the point where having Dad around wasn't necessary. Now, seven years later, we're a little happier, but

The righteous man leads a blameless life; blessed are his children after him.

He who fears the Lord has a secure fortress, and for his children it will be a refuge.

Train a child in the way he should go, and when he is old he will not turn from it.

Proverbs

it's not anything like I wish it could be. I missed my chance, *and now it's too late.*"

More evidence is popping up these days that fast-track fathers are rethinking the cost of climbing the corporate ladder. Robert Half International conducted a survey that asked respondents, "Would you be likely to accept a promotion involving greater responsibility if it meant spending less time with your family?"

Only one-third answered yes, while most replied no (55 percent). The rest were not sure. In September 1991, the *Wall Street Journal* reported on a fatherhood survey of three hundred executives and middle managers. One father's statement stood out: "Ten years ago I told my wife and children to just wait until I get established, and then I could spend more time with them. Now that I want to get involved with them, I am finding they're more comfortable *without* me."

That's right, Dad. If you're not around, your wife and children will learn to live life without you. It's as if you're the manager of the New York Yankees, but you don't arrive at the ballpark until the seventh inning. You'll find the players and coaches playing the game without you. Life goes on.

Not every dad who feels he must pour his best years into his work (or has a job that forces him to travel) will end up with a lifetime of regret. (If you do have to travel, we'll provide a few ideas on how to stay close to your kids. That's later in this chapter.) But these stories are meant to illustrate this point: We're only given a short time with our children, and the best years to get them on our team are when they're young.

A slightly adjusted passage from the New Testament strikes the nail on the head. "What would it profit a man if he gain the whole world, but lose his own kids?"

> "That's right, Dad. If you're not around, your wife and children will learn to live life without you."

MEN AND THEIR KIDS

Don't Make It Up as You Go

So, what makes a good dad?

That was the opening question during our interviews, an ice-breaker designed to put our fathers at ease. Some dads dipped their toes into the water before warming to the subject; others dove in headfirst. Invariably, however, nearly all the fathers stressed the importance of spending time with their children.

Of course, that's the no-brainer answer we expected—and wanted—to hear from fathers who are getting the job done. The importance of spending time with your children is an altruism that needs to be repeated as much as possible. Time is a nonrenewable resource; once it's gone, it's gone.

"I'm a big believer in time with the kids," says Charles, an investment counselor. "I think the time commitment you make when they are younger reaps dividends later on."

Alex, from Omaha, believes the key is delegating his time properly. "I make sure I have individual time and corporate time with my children. It's easy to forget the younger kids because they can be caught up in the shadow of the older ones," said the father of six.

Alex has three teens (ages thirteen to seventeen) and three younger ones (ages four to nine). "It's like having two families," he says. "It's important to get down at eye level and listen to them. It doesn't matter what we do, as long as we do something. It doesn't have to be something stupendous. Sometimes we just do family pantomime on a winter's evening."

Another father, Jonathan, also schedules individual time with each of his children. "We'll play baseball, go to a movie, or bowl," he says. "I want to be sure I can communicate with them. We can talk about what's on their minds or what's bothering them. I want to grow with my children so that when

"Time is a nonrenewable resource; once it's gone, it's gone."

MEN AND THEIR KIDS

a crisis does occur, they will feel comfortable enough to come to me to talk about it."

Some Hard Facts

The Family Research Council, a division of Focus on the Family based in Washington, D.C., analyzes research regarding the family. A recent FRC finding revealed that parents are spending 40 percent less time with their children than they did twenty-five years ago. In the midsixties an average parent spent thirty hours a week with a child. Today, the average parent spends only seventeen hours.

Studies from two University of Michigan economists (who reviewed time diaries over two decades) buttress this "time famine" information. Out of a 168-hour week, American men on the average devoted fifty-six hours to work, seventy hours to sleeping, eating, and personal care, and forty-two hours to leisure activities.

Another time-use study from the University of Maryland broke down the figures even further. Every twenty-four hours (figuring in weekdays and weekends), men spend

- 7 hours and 50 minutes sleeping
- 1 hour and 15 minutes eating
- 30 minutes grooming
- 1 hour and 45 minutes on household chores
- 7 hours and 10 minutes working
- 5 hours and 30 minutes on leisure activities

Notice the last entry: five-and-a-half hours for leisure activities. That roughly matches up with what we said earlier about what the most important hours of the day are—the hours between 5:00 and 10:00 P.M.

MEN AND THEIR KIDS

52

Taking Stock

Let's do a little exercise: Grab a pencil and determine how you "spent" your last twenty-four hours (make it a weekday):

Sleeping _____

Grooming _____

Working (main job) _____

Commuting _____

Overtime or moonlighting _____

Household chores _____

Eating with the family _____

Leisure pursuits _____
    (exercise, reading, hobbies)

After you've added up the hours, ask yourself these questions:

- Was this a routine day?
- How much time did I spend with my children?
- What did I do with them?
- Was I home for dinner?
- Did I do paperwork while Mom bathed the kids and put them down?
- Did I talk with my wife?
- How much time was frittered away watching TV?

These questions are not meant to heap guilt on you, but to help you take stock. Not surprisingly, Americans believe "parents having less time to spend with their families" is the single most important reason for the family's decline in our society, according to a 1989 survey commissioned by the Massachusetts Mutual Insurance Company.

The average five-year-old, we are told, spends twenty-five *minutes* a week in close interaction with

MEN AND THEIR KIDS

"Parents having less time to spend with their families is the single most important reason for the family's decline in our society."

his father and twenty-five *hours* a week in close inter-action with the TV. No wonder that in a recent survey of kindergartners and their priorities, Dad finished second to the boob tube.

The moral of the story? If we're not committed to our children, we can't expect them to be committed to us.

One thing to keep in mind when pollsters and research centers conduct these surveys is that they don't monitor the really important stuff: how many times a parent hugs a child or how often a father volunteers to coach a team. Nor is there anyone keeping track of how effectively values are passed on at the dinner table and at bedtime or how long a family is on their knees each night praying to the God they love.

When's the last time you cheered on your daughter's soccer team? Have you taken the family on a recent after-dinner stroll through the neighborhood? When's the last time you did something unexpected, such as taking your children to a parade, the zoo, or even Chuck E. Cheese's?

> "If we're not committed to our children, we can't expect them to be committed to us."

MEN AND THEIR KIDS

Some Ideas

If you agree that spending time with our kids is a great idea—right up there with ordering a hot dog at a ball game—how can you do it? Here are some ideas our fifty fathers shared with us.

Rearranging Your Work Schedule

If possible, rearrange your work schedule. Herb is an orthopedic surgeon in Akron, Ohio. At forty-three, Herb is getting his practice established, but he knows the medical profession can gobble up hours in huge chunks.

"How do I spend time with my kids?" asked Herb. "I'm not a morning person, so I've changed my hours around. That way, I don't have to go into the office right away. I can eat breakfast with my kids and take them to school. I start my surgeries at one o'clock in the afternoon and go until 7:00 P.M. or so."

Herb isn't home often for dinner, but he's there for breakfast. And how many fathers can say they drive their children to school?

"I also take every Tuesday afternoon off, and last summer, I began a long-term project with my kids— building a fort," he says. A creek runs through the back of his property, and his elementary-age children love to pound nails and watch Dad cut plywood. "We're building the fort because the children want to build it. I also don't play golf or tennis with the guys in the office. I'm either working around the house or with my family. That's the only way I can spend time with them," he says.

Notice that Herb said he doesn't have time for friendships outside the family. Many of the fathers we interviewed said they've had to make the same choice, too. In our survey, 50 percent of the fathers said they spend one hour or less each week with close friends outside of work.

Understanding the Breadth of Life

"After we lost our oldest son in a drowning accident," said one father from Alabama, "I really started living one day at a time. I lived as though it was the last time I'd see each child. When I'm with them now, I try to make every time meaningful."

Making Dinnertime a Priority

Dinner is a time to reconnect. A poll conducted by *Parents of Teenagers* magazine found that out of twenty-one meals a week, nearly one-third said they eat fewer than five meals together as a family. And only one-fourth of families even eat together half the time.

There's something about the entire family sitting around and enjoying a meal together. And in this day and age of working moms, long commutes, and kids in sports, sharing a meal is no easy goal.

Top Seven Worst Ways To Spend Time with Your Kids

7 Serve as their human quarter machine at the video arcade.

6 Have the NBA game of the week on while you're playing Monopoly with them.

5 Read the paper while helping them with their algebra assignments.

4 Go to the local high school football field to practice your short-irons and have them collect the golf balls after you're done.

3 Suggest they take a nap with you on a beautiful Sunday afternoon.

2 Drive them to Cub Scouts and read a magazine in the car while the den mother instructs them on how to tie knots.

1 Take them to your office on Saturday and have them color while you work.

Eating together promotes communication, which promotes discussion, which promotes sharing, which promotes love. Did you ever notice that when you eat alone you flip on the TV? You want some sort of communication, even if it's one way.

Dinnertime together is also a great way to know what's going on in your kids' lives. Brad, a New England father, says that when the family sits down each

MEN AND THEIR KIDS

night, he asks each child, "What was the best thing that happened to you today?"

"Doing that stimulates talk, and everyone has to listen," says Brad. "That way, you begin the dinner conversation with a positive focus, and I try to remember something the kids said so when it's time for nightly prayer, I can say 'Thanks, Lord, for helping Jeremy pass the test.'"

In the last year, Brad has tried to spend some unscheduled time with his kids, too. Sometimes he'll knock on the bedroom door and ask to come in and just talk. "It's amazing how kids will open up then," he says.

Banning the TV

What book worth its salt wouldn't suggest this? But letting the hours vaporize into thin air because the "boob tube" drones on and on *is* a waste of time. Apparently, the fathers we interviewed agreed. Nearly one-third (29 percent) said they don't watch any TV during the week, and 61 percent said they watch one to two hours a night, a manageable figure. So, nine out of ten dads have the TV under control.

"We don't watch TV on weeknights," says one father. "We made a commitment not to. Instead, we read or play games in the basement, such as 'hand baseball' with a Nerf ball."

A Regular Family Time

Sometimes Howard brings a calendar to the dinner table, and then he and the family block off one night a month, usually a Friday, for fun and games. Other fathers we talked to said they reserve a Saturday or Sunday for their families.

Family Nights—or Family Days—are not a new invention; we've heard of many families incorporating this idea. Often it serves as a buffer for busy parents

MEN AND THEIR KIDS

"Letting the hours vaporize into thin air because the 'boob tube' drones on and on is a waste of time."

whose lives are caught up in soccer leagues, music lessons, and carpools. Putting aside one evening or day each week can provide an important haven for the entire family. It also promotes togetherness.

"I specifically put aside one day a week," says Tim, "and once we've set the day, I'll say no to things. Generally, it's a weeknight, but it can be a Saturday. For family fun, we'll go on a drive or feed ducks at a pond. It really doesn't have to be a high-energy thing. We might just get an ice cream."

"Daddy Dates"

Westy, a Wisconsin father, says he can think of nothing better than taking his nine-year-old daughter out

Being a Good Dad When You're on the Road

"GOD'S ROLE FOR THE FATHER as head of the home should be the norm for families, yet in millions of households, Dad won't be home tonight." So wrote Paul Lewis in "Long Distance Dads," a story we once ran in *Focus on the Family* magazine. We're seeing more and more fathers who must travel for days at a time. If you have to be out of town, here are some things you can do:

- The night before you leave on a business trip, organize a treasure hunt for the kids. The "treasure" doesn't have to be something material, but it could be a personalized letter that shares your love for them.

- Call home every day. One man says, "The phone calls don't have to be long, especially if you really can't afford them, but hearing your voice every day is essential for the family to stay connected to each other."

MEN AND THEIR KIDS

- Do something special with each child before you leave for the trip. Some fathers promise to a special outing upon their return, but . . . it never works out. If you have individual time with your child before you depart *and* you do something when you get home, you'll be on your way to making up lost time.

  Another good idea is to make a tape of you reading a bedtime story, which your wife can play as the children fall asleep.

- If your trip is a long one, send postcards or letters each day. Some dads even mail their kids a card before they leave so they'll have something in the mailbox the first day Dad's gone. (The first day is always the roughest.)

- While a present from each trip may be a must for you, don't believe gifts can soften the blow of your not being around. You can't buy your child's love.

- Cancel or shorten a few business trips (if possible) and tell your kids you did it because you couldn't stand leaving them again. In their little minds, children sometimes reason that Dad's leaving because he doesn't like them or they've done something wrong. Telling them that you're staying just for them will build their confidence in you.

  Some fathers cut their trips short by returning home late at night instead of staying one more night and catching a flight home the next day. Even if they arrive home just before midnight—bushed—they're home. Then they can eat breakfast with the family (and most likely, they don't have to hurry into the office).

for breakfast or dinner. "She knows the only reason we're going out is so we can talk," says Westy. "We probably get as much conversation in during that one meal as we do all week. We sit across the table from each other and converse; there are a lot of questions and answers going on. These 'Daddy Dates' tell my daughter that she is very, very important to me."

A good time to start "dating" your child is around eight or nine years old. "Don't wait until he or she is fifteen years old. That's too late," says Westy. By spending individual time with your child, you build a friendship, so when the *really* big discussions pop up later (love, dating, and sex), a foundation has already been laid.

Vacations

You'd be surprised at the number of families who vacation without their kids. Mac is a sixty-seven-year-old grandfather from Southern California who has never regretted including his four sons in all the family vacations.

"When the boys were between the ages of five and fifteen, we did a lot of camping, boating, fishing, and waterskiing," says Mac. One evening, when his oldest son, Todd, was eighteen, he had a suggestion for the family: "Why don't we go around the world?"

The year was 1972, and Mac's construction business was going great guns. Why not take an extended trip? Todd was about to graduate. His brother, Tommy, could continue his high school education by correspondence. And the two younger boys, Keith and Denny, well, they would just have to miss a year of school.

The first stop was in Rome, and from the Eternal City, the family made its way south and east, traveling through North Africa, Israel, and the Middle East. Usually they spent two weeks at each stop, staying in cheap motels and shopping at the local markets. The last half of the trip took them through India, Sri Lanka, and several South Pacific islands, where they slept in grass huts.

"We really saw how other cultures lived," says Mac, "and it sure made the kids appreciative of what they had. It's too bad all families can't afford it because it was the most rewarding thing we did as a family. Now my sons all want to do it with their children."

Really?

We called Todd, now thirty-seven, and asked if that was true.

"Sure, I would love to do that with my kids, but I'm not sure if it will ever work out," he replied. "But I'm open to the Lord's leading. Because of that around-the-world trip, my brother Denny decided to go into full-time medical missions service. It was a real eye-opening experience," says Todd.

When Randy, a Texas rancher, and his family go on vacation, they drive. That way, Randy's certain they'll have plenty of time in the car. (Believe it or not, that's the way he wants it!) One of the kids sits with Dad in the front seat, and as the scenery passes by, long discussions ensue.

"We use that time in the car to visit with each other," says Randy. "I've had both kids tell me that it's fun to drive together and see the country."

Coaching

Volunteer to coach your child's sports team. When you make that commitment to coach, it forces you to spend time with your children. That's the way Jeffrey, a Sacramento father, slices out hours with his four children (ranging in age from three to fifteen). He's coached baseball for eight years, from Little League through Pony League. "Baseball is a real competitive sport here in California, and with a lot of competition comes a lot of pressure. There's a struggle to keep sports in the right perspective. I tell my boys to use the talents the Lord gives them—but to have fun, too. I think the lessons sports teach are good for kids because they learn about life's ups and downs," says Jeffrey.

"In order to spend time with my kids," says Cedric, a Kansas accountant, "I coach various sports teams, like baseball and basketball. I go to school functions. I help them with their homework. I help them study for their tests."

Cedric keeps a little sign on his desk. It reads: "The best thing you can spend on your children is time."

"That's a nice reminder for me," he says.

Cheering from the Grandstand

If you can't be a coach, then cheer from the grandstand. Max, an attorney, said he always wanted to take time to be with Max, Jr., while he was growing up, but Max, Sr., wasn't the athletic type.

"I didn't coach, but I went to all the Little League games where I could encourage him. And when he started playing high school football, I was there, even for his JV games that started at 3:00 P.M. I was lucky to have a job with flexible hours."

Max received the biggest compliment any dad could hope for when his son married a couple of years ago. As the church organ pumped the "Wedding March" and the various attendants walked down the center aisle, Max, Jr., made small talk with the pastor in the vestibule.

"I want to be like my dad," the bridegroom said. "I want to do it right."

"What I took from that," said the proud pop afterward, "is that he wants a Christian home just like his father. That's the key: spending time and being involved in *their* interests."

One father in the Chicago area told us his neighbors ask him why he has extraordinary kids. "What's your secret?" they say.

He replies that he and his wife had made an early commitment to go to *everything* at school—recitals,

MEN AND THEIR KIDS

sports, band concerts, you name it. "Even if the kids tell you they don't want you to show up, they really do," says the Windy City dad.

Maximizing Recreational Time

Make the best use of your recreational time. It's important to exercise our bodies (we feel better when we're in good shape). Many of us enjoy the spirit of competition. Some recreational pursuits, however, take up a lot of time.

Take golf, for instance. As Baby Boomers age, golf is *the* sport of the nineties. Yet when I (Mike) play, it burns up most of a Saturday. Even if I'm a member of the "dawn patrol," I'm still not home till noon. I've decided golf is going to have to wait; I'm lucky if I play three rounds a year.

That's why I play a lot of tennis, but I've had to cut back there, too. Usually, I'll play one or two mornings a week before work, starting at 6:30 A.M. I figure it's better to play while the kids are still sleeping than to practice my forehand after work when they're home. Greg plays basketball before work for the same reasons.

If I do play a match after work, I'll try to squeeze in a 5:15 match, telling my opponent that I can play only for an hour because I have to get home for dinner. Many of my tennis buddies ask me to drink an iced tea and chat after our game, but I politely say, "No, thanks. I gotta get home to my family."

"Do household chores together. There's something about pulling weeds, trimming lawns, and tidying up that brings a family together."

Working Around the House

Do household chores together. There's something about pulling weeds, trimming lawns, and tidying up that brings a family together—you know "The family that works together, stays together."

"Working in the yard was something we did as a family," says Mac, the father who took his four sons on the around-the-world trip. "Now our boys have a great love for gardening." A well-kept garden also makes the house look great and can give the entire family a sense of pride.

Remembering That Your Kids Are Keeping Tabs on You

When fifteen hundred schoolchildren were asked by social scientists John DeFrain and Nick Stinnett, "What do you think makes a happy family?" the children didn't list money, fine homes, or big-screen TVs. No, the answer most frequently offered was "doing things together."

"I once saw a sign in the nursery," said Herbert, the fort-building physician. "It said: 'Children spell love t-i-m-e.' You can't buy your kids' affection unless you spend your time with them."

Man to Man

1. If you could relive your last twenty-four hours, what changes would you make?

2. Identify activities you have shared with your children in the past week. Which of these helped you to feel closer to the children—and to your wife?

3. Select one new activity to share with your child/children and decide when you might do it and what you hope to accomplish.

MEN AND THEIR KIDS

5

HOPELESSLY DEVOTED OR HOPELESS DEVOTIONS?

Men and Their God

What are the Top Ten reasons men don't pray more often?

10 We fall asleep after saying, "Now I lay me down to sleep . . . "

9 We're so bushed by the end of the day that we usually doze off by 8:30 P.M.

8 Why pray when we can worry?

7 We're either on the freeway or watching a football game when CNN reports the bad news we could pray for.

6 We secretly hope that if we keep quiet, God won't know what we've been up to.

5 So many cable channels, so little time.

If you remain in me and my words remain in you, ask whatever you wish, and it will be given you.
John

4 We have a bad tendency to fall over backward when kneeling (which might lead to stretching—which could lead to exercise!).

3 April 15 comes only once a year.

2 The wife snores.

1 The Chicago Cubs never win the N.L. pennant.

You know, this subject is way too convicting to cover this early in a book. Let's hit a few other topics first and get back to it in chapter 13.

MEN AND THEIR GOD

6

MAKING THE WIFE FEEL GOOD

(No, This Isn't the Chapter on Sex)

Men and Their Mates

*H*ow do I look?"

I (Mike) barely glanced over the edge of my newspaper as Nicole walked into the family room.

"Fine, honey," I said, hurrying back to the box scores. (My San Diego Padres were battling another losing streak.)

"Don't you think I look nice?"

I guess I'm not going to get away so easy after all. I put the paper down and gave her my undivided attention.

"You look very nice, Nicole," I said, trying to sound as though I meant it. She always looks nice. But she doesn't believe me when I tell her that. "Really, that outfit looks great on you. You look great."

"Yeah, right."

"No, really."

And there goes another round of communication between my wife and me. If there is one thing I have learned through the years, it's that I definitely have to notice how Nicole is dressed before we go out in the

Husbands, in the same way be considerate as you live with your wives, and treat them with respect as the weaker partner and as heirs with you of the gracious gift of life, so that nothing will hinder your prayers.

1 Peter

evening. I don't have to praise her, but life sure goes better when I do.

I'm sure Nicole is like millions of other wives. Don't ask me why, but it takes her a good sixty minutes to shower and shave her legs, slap lotion over her body, blow-dry her hair, pluck her eyebrows, file her nails, powder her nose, fix her eyes, and get dressed. I can get showered and changed in ten minutes flat, eight if I'm in a hurry.

When Nicole invests one hour in looking good, she wants to hear my approval—several times over. And that's fine with me. The problem is it took me almost ten years to figure it out.

Romancing our wives and being good husbands are part of the most important hours of the day for today's fathers. So is the all-important physical relationship, which is why Greg and I are devoting the next three chapters to providing practical ideas for enhancing the love between a husband and wife.

Homegrown Lessons

The more I (Mike) learn about building my wife's self-esteem, the more I wonder how I got through my first decade of marriage. Nicole is a stay-at-home mom for the most part. Naturally, much of her self-esteem is tied up in how she raises the children, looks in the mirror, keeps the house, prepares the meals, and plays tennis (she's pretty good).

I try to do little things to let her know I've noticed. Okay, so I'm no Kevin Costner, but I bring her flowers, empty the dishwasher, and take the kids off her hands when I can.

All of that so she'll be putty in my hands after the kids go to bed, right? *Wrong!* Most likely, our wives will be too pooped to do much of anything after

MEN AND THEIR MATES

the kids are down. They're often frazzled and worn out by the time they get to relax.

But we've got other ideas. *Hey, maybe if I take the garbage out she'll slip into that little negligée . . .*

Whenever we talked to men who'd been married for more than ten years, you could almost hear them slap their foreheads. "No one told me that women aren't like men when it comes to romance!"

Like the other guys, I wasted years of doing little things in the name of romance when all Nicole really wanted was for me to treat her like a real, valuable person.

Cherish Is the Word

Unless you wrote your own vows in the hippy-dippy sixties or disco-happy seventies, you probably promised God and the assembled wedding guests that you would cherish the woman whose eyes you were intently gazing into. Yet somewhere between the wedding vows and the honeymoon bed our hormones shifted into overdrive. The promise to "cherish and to hold" was quickly forgotten during the rapid transition into married life.

It's usually years later before we wonder if we could have done more to build her up, to cherish her, as we promised we would. Perhaps we need a reminder of the word's definition from Webster's: *"cher-ish: 1. hold dear; feel or show love for; 2. to take good care of; protect; 3. to cling to the idea or feeling of. Syn. see appreciate."*

To which many wives will say, "Yeah, let's see some appreciation around here."

It's not that we never do nice things for our wives. We love and serve, yet during our times of sexual romance, she's looking to be cherished. Do you see the difference? You can bet your last paycheck your wife does!

"Romancing our wives and being good husbands are part of the most important hours of the day for today's fathers."

In case the point still isn't clear, heartfelt romance (cherishing) does not equal hormone romance (you know what we mean). And believe us, our wives can distinguish between the two.

Picture-Perfect Wives

If you're a well-read, Bible-type guy, you're sure that God loves your wife unconditionally. She is without spot or blame. God knit every fiber of her body together, and He values her enough to have died on a Cross for her. If Christ treasures her, you should too. And if your wife truly understands all these concepts, she'll automatically feel wonderful about herself because "God said it; I believe it; that settles it."

Though such an a+b=c approach might work for men, it rarely works that way for women. We conducted a small, secondary survey of fathers attending a men's retreat, and one of the questions we asked was "Does your wife have a low self-image?"

Ninety-five percent said yes or somewhat. The men said they noticed their wives doing the following behavior:

- She puts herself down (60 percent of the men gave this as a symptom).
- She doesn't initiate close friendships with other women (45 percent).
- She's a perfectionist with the kids (40 percent).
- She doesn't initiate romance for fear of rejection (35 percent).
- She's unable to receive compliments (25 percent).
- She's often bored (20 percent).
- She puts me down in front of friends (5 percent).
- She refuses to confront life's major issues (5 percent).

MEN AND THEIR MATES

The Less-Than-Helpful Responses

Well, guys, what can we do about it? Let's flip this question on its head and look over the following responses.

"What's in It for Me?"

"Since I'm under thirty, my high-potency sexual years are still in full swing, so it's okay to expect something in return for 'cherishing-type' behavior."

If you want a vibrant sex life in your thirties and forties, you'd better start cherishing! This is a lesson you can't learn too early. Sexual selfishness may appear to have short-term benefits, but it's definitely a bad long-term strategy. Through nonverbal and verbal communication, men must love women as Christ loved the church—from courtship to well beyond the fiftieth wedding anniversary. So back off on hormone romance and refocus your efforts on cherishing your wife.

"Give It Time"

"My wife's low self-esteem will eventually correct itself through time and a growing relationship with Christ."

As long as magazines, movies, and TV present an unrealistic picture of females, women will always struggle with comparisons. They literally can never measure up to 37-24-36. The hourglass figure is ingrained in them from their days of playing with Barbie dolls. "One thing that bugs me is the emphasis our society places on beauty and looks," said one father. Another husband said he tells his wife he loves her body no matter what. That will lift her self-esteem!

Marty always tells his wife, Katrina, how beautiful she is. "That makes her feel wonderful," he says. "The whole church knows she's a terrible cook, but I'll say it doesn't matter. I tell her I married her for her great legs. I'm always telling others how much I love her."

"Heartfelt romance (cherishing) does not equal hormone romance (you know what we mean). And believe us, our wives can distinguish between the two."

"It's All in Her Head"

"I'm not part of the problem. Low self-esteem is all in her head."

Like many successful men, Mark is an intense competitor. "I grew up where performance was everything," said the Kentucky father. "I've always tried to measure things with a scorecard of some type. That way I could determine if I did better than anyone else. I finished a stress test for my heart a while back, and the doctors told me I was in very good physical condition. My response? 'How long would I have to stay on this treadmill to get an excellent rating?'

"I had three brothers; my wife had four sisters," continued Mark. "Her family was raised to keep it all inside. When it came to our relationship, I was overbearing, but she was passive. It was tough since she felt as though she never measured up, especially since I didn't have a clue how to treat a woman. We've considered counseling, but we've never gone."

Men who contribute to their wives' poor self-concept usually have no clue that they're part of the problem. A man whose wife has self-image difficulties *needs* to be part of the solution. If he's not sure how to proceed, he should ask a neutral party how he can get started in the right direction. Until Mark has the humility to seek help, he's as likely to build up his wife as a college student is likely to engineer a high-rise building.

"Saying Is Believing"

"If my wife often hears me say how I feel about her, she'll change her way of thinking."

Not always. An Ohio journalist says it's his tendency to try to patch things up with his wife right away, as if he had a deadline to meet. "I told her, 'Hey, just feel better about yourself,'" said Robert. "Instead of listening and being a sounding board, I want

72

to take a crowbar to the situation and pry open a solution. A good example happened the other day when
my wife said she was three pounds overweight. My
'sensitive' response was something like 'Compare
yourself to other women—you're doing great.' And
there she goes feeling sorry for herself. Then she feels
bad, and then feels bad that she feels bad. Then she'll
go eat and really feel bad."

Yikes! Within a woman's life are constant reminders of her "unworthiness": a perfectionist mother
whom she's still trying to please; a sister who got all
the looks and most of the personality; girlfriends from
high school or college who "married well" and are living in upscale neighborhoods; women at church who
look and act so "together"; her mother-in-law, who
can send subtle signals that she's not "good enough";
and the perky, attractive women at your office who
are always so friendly.

"Hugs Aren't That Important"

*"I can lighten up on the physical affection because all she
really needs is cherishing."*

Just as you need physical closeness to feel like a
man, she needs to express her womanhood with you,
both for her emotional needs and to feel good about
herself as a wife.

Well, what else can you do?

You can:

- back off (give her some space)
- be patient (don't rush things)
- love her as you love your own body (that's
  going to take some work)
- affirm her role in the family (whether she stays
  home or works outside the home, she's got the
  most important job in the world)
- pray for her as you've never prayed before (because God hears our prayers)

- lower your expectations (you're not going to see fireworks every night)
- do the little things (without expecting anything in return)
- show her she's the most cherished woman on earth (she'll probably faint the first time you do this)
- above all, persevere (you're in this for the long haul)

Flowers and Notes

A business owner from upstate New York has been building his wife's self-esteem for twenty-one years. Shortly after Charles married Cynthia, he gradually realized that his bride was a product of an oppressive childhood. They sought counseling, and it helped. "My wife needs ten times more lifting up and appreciating than I ever would have guessed," said Charles. "In a genuine fashion I've lavished calls, notes, and flowers on her for no particular reason. It's slowly working."

Charles is a patient man. Perhaps some of you know what it's like to marry a woman whom the world would consider "damaged goods." Our challenge is to give of ourselves so she will feel like "treasured goods" one day.

Let's not paint too dark a picture. Not every woman brings major baggage to the marriage, and some who do may need just a short time before they're empowered by the confidence we and God build into them. A woman who's comfortable with herself is more likely to be honest, less fearful of rejection, more communicative, and perhaps (though this isn't the goal, remember) more desirous of romantic intimacy.

MEN AND THEIR MATES

Start with the Little Things

We asked our men what they do to build up or romance their wives. In case you're wondering, bringing her flowers was the number one reply. Not terribly original, but it's worked for several thousand years, right guys?

"We have a good marriage," says Bart, a Toledo man. "I buy her flowers, make her laugh, and treat her like a schoolgirl. We're affectionate in front of our kids, although it makes the older ones gag. But both our parents were that way."

Today's moms need strokes and plenty of hugs. Why? Because society, for the most part, is not giving mothers, especially stay-at-home moms, their due. Everywhere a mom looks in today's society, she's being told that she's behind the moon if she's not working outside the home. When's the last time you saw a women's magazine or "Donahue" tell their readers or viewers that staying home and raising the kids is the best way to go?

"How do I build self-esteem in my wife?" asks Terry, a high school history teacher from Colorado. "I try to remind her that the task she is doing, being a stay-at-home mom, is the most important task God has given her. I let her know that I appreciate what she's doing. I'll surprise her now and then with flowers, and I'll leave love notes around the house."

"Today's moms need strokes and plenty of hugs."

Just as creative is Kevin, who writes poems to his wife, Sandy. "To my embarrassment, she's kept every one of them," he laughs.

But we're probably a lot like Michael, who says he takes his wife for granted. "Sometimes I feel as though I don't tell her I love her enough. Perhaps I'm too busy with other things. Anyway, I think many husbands have the same problem. My wife, Erica, likes to hear the words 'I love you' and to have her hand held and her body hugged."

Michael says when life gets too hectic—she's carpooling the kids to school and after-school appointments while his work backs up—their relationship takes a nosedive. "When we're going in opposite directions, the opportunity to communicate is not there."

Bruce, who lives in Chicago, says that with four kids, he and his wife have to fight for any time together. "I will be the first to admit that three, four years ago the kids were much more demanding. That was before any of them could drive, and they were going to different schools. It seems as though we were driving them everywhere."

Now Bruce and his wife get up at 5:30 A.M., and the two of them read their Bibles and talk. "When Suzanne wants to chat, I don't always have to talk. Sometimes she's just ventilating a problem. If I say, 'Okay, here's how you solve that,' that's not what she wants. She just wants someone to talk to and bounce ideas off of."

A Houston father told us his wife opens up when he initiates spending time with her. "She also loves it when I do some of the dusting and bathroom cleaning," says Russell. "It makes her feel like she's not a housekeeper. What really bursts her bubble is when I come home all wrapped up in work. It's something we talk about, and when things aren't well, she'll make me aware I'm slipping into treating work as more important than she."

Raymond says he makes it a point to tell his wife about his day. "She likes that," says Ray, "since letting her know what's going on in my life is a bridge between us. We often talk after dinner or after the kids are in bed. To do that, we don't allow the television on during the week. That's been a hard rule to put into effect, but it's been very rewarding to our family." The no-TV rule also promotes lingering dinner discussions, according to Ray, since no one is in a hurry to leave the table.

Taking conversation to the next level has proved to be just the trick for a Florida lawyer. "It's taken a while," says Roberto, "but just as I want to support my wife in her areas of weakness, I'm allowing her to support me in mine. When she ministers to me, she feels important and special. While it kind of goes against my nature to let people that close, it's really boosted how she feels about herself. And you know, she's really helped me sort out my feelings about work and life in general."

Another father counseled, "When your wife is talking, look at her and enjoy what she's saying. You can just tell there's a sparkle in her eye when you're building her up in public."

On Our Shoulders

One way Helmut builds up his wife is to take the pressure of the family finances off her shoulders. Helmut says more and more busy husbands are asking their wives to pay the bills, balance the checkbook, and keep track of the family budget. Not him.

"I make sure my wife is relieved of those pressures," says Helmut. "None of those things are her problems. If the car breaks, for instance, I'll say, 'Hey, I'll get it fixed. That's my responsibility.'"

Helmut tells the story about a wife who was driving the family van when an electrical fire started, destroying the car. Her husband could have blathered "You idiot," but instead, he took full responsibility for the burned-up vehicle. He secured a replacement car and dealt with the insurance company, taking the load off her shoulders.

You can bet his wife thinks the world of her husband.

The same goes for husbands who set the spiritual pace for their wives and families. Chris, a parachurch development director from Wisconsin, says, "Part of my responsibility as a husband is to bring out my wife's gifts and encourage her to use them for the kingdom. If I treat her as a fellow heir, then we don't have to compete. She can feel good knowing God is using her in a significant way. I have to be aware of her priorities and serve as God's surrogate cheerleader so she'll have the courage to use her many gifts."

One father said he's noticed that his attitude toward his wife improves when he prays for her. "I ask God to give her wisdom for raising the kids and managing the household," says Kyle. "I pray that I will be captivated by her love and that I will be satisfied with her physical body. That's an area for me to think about. You see, then my focus is on her. When I pray that way every week, it helps our marriage a lot."

Taking the initiative for morning prayer with his wife has helped Adrian, who lives in Montana. "No matter how tired or stressed out we are, when we pray, we're really rewarded. Our communication with each other is much better, and I can understand her feelings more when we pray through family trials."

No Quick Fixes

To repeat: Building your wife's self-esteem is something to be done over the long haul, and if you've built her up over the years brick by brick, your sunset years will be much brighter. "It hit home with me a little while ago," said Leon. "It's not going to be too long before all the kids are going to leave the house. My wife and I are going to have to be good friends with mutual interests because once the kids are gone, it's just her and me."

Man to Man

1. Identify some things you have learned over the years of your marriage about your wife's particular needs.

2. Discuss some ways that you might be able to cherish your wife as you promised in your marriage vows.

3. List the qualities that you want in a good friend. Which of these qualities do you want to nurture in your wife?

MEN AND THEIR MATES

7

TAKING YOUR WIFE TO COURT

Men and Romance

*F*riday night is Date Night for Ronnie and Rhonda. After a long week, their dates are a time to unwind, take stock, and reconnect, a chance to ease into the weekend.

Ronnie calls himself the "Master of the Cheap Date." But don't get the wrong idea. A CPA by trade, Ronnie has taught finance seminars at their local church, and he and his wife have counseled couples on financial matters. "We often describe the difference between being good stewards and being cheap," said Ronnie, "and that difference is learning how to be careful with the money we spend on food, clothing, and ourselves."

Actually, Ronnie is the "Master of the Thrifty Date." A cheapskate, he says, is one who orders the least expensive thing on the menu and then stiffs the waitress out of a tip. "That's not a good witness either," he adds.

Let's follow this happy couple on a typical Friday night out on the town. They usually drive over to a Vons Pavilions (a Southern California upscale super-market/deli) and order a Chinese takeout platter for

May your fountain be blessed, and may you rejoice in the wife of your youth.

Proverbs

five bucks. Then they carry their meal to one of the two plastic tables in front of the supermarket.

Invariably, church friends wave at—and razz—the couple as they walk into Vons. "Hey, Ronnie!" yells one friend. "Got your wife out on a date, I see."

Ronnie and Rhonda share a laugh, but only because they know one couple who are even cheaper. "We know this guy who took his wife to the blood bank on Tuesday nights. Why? Because that's when they feed you free for donating blood. Now, that's *cheap.* No way am I going to give blood to get a free dinner," says Ronnie.

"By scheduling a regular date night, he's telling Rhonda (in his own unique style) that he loves her, that she's special enough to court."

Starry, Starry Night

But Ronnie's on the right track. By scheduling a regular date night, he's telling Rhonda (in his own unique style) that he loves her, that she's special enough to court. Friday night dates are a weekly reminder that he values her company and wants to communicate with her over egg rolls and chow mein.

Ronnie has an even better surefire way to romance his wife: rolling up his shirtsleeves and attacking the dinner dishes. "Twice a week I wash the dishes and clean up the kitchen," says Ronnie. "I tell Rhonda, 'Honey, go sit on the couch and kick up your feet.' Then I get the boys, and we clean up the dinner dishes. I tell them we're treating Mom special tonight."

Isn't that the point behind any service we do?

Are there other ways we can treat our spouses special? We're glad you asked. As we emphasized in the last chapter, you must adjust your attitude about relating to your wife. Read our lips: The "little woman" was not created to do our sexual bidding.

MEN AND ROMANCE

When we vowed to cherish and love her, that meant she became more important than our own bodies.

When the Honeymoon's Over

After a young couple have exchanged their wedding vows and cut the cake, they sometimes make a hasty exit for the getaway car. Once they're on the way, the couple enjoy a two-week honeymoon, followed by a season of marital bliss.

But after a few months, or maybe a year or two, young couples often experience a low period. In fact, some get stuck in marital ruts—you know, those traps you've got to push and shove to get out of. Ask any five- to ten-year marital vet, and he'll tell you how they develop:

- Communication being reduced to yes and no answers or occurring only when you're trying to read each other's minds
- Busyness due to too many hours on the job
- Minor resentments being allowed to build into larger ones
- Busyness due to a higher commitment to outside activities, including church commitments
- Minor offenses or cross words going without an apology and therefore unforgiven
- Busyness due to an overactive social schedule
- Children demanding a lot of attention
- Lack of money because financial priorities are built around acquiring possessions instead of making memories

Funny, but when I (Greg) was first married, I never believed my romance meter would head toward zero. *Our marriage will always have the spark necessary to withstand any distractions,* I thought. But I didn't

MEN AND ROMANCE

"When we vowed to cherish and love her, that meant she became more important than our own bodies."

even notice when I failed to carry on a real conversation with Elaine for weeks at a time. Oh sure, we talked about some things—the kids, my job, her work—but we never discussed our struggles or the frustrations she faced with two toddlers.

I unconsciously convinced myself that I didn't have the energy to let her inside my world, so I didn't. Simple as that. While I still craved physical attention, I never gave a thought to giving her any emotional attention. Life got pretty selfish.

Yet all around me, there were little reminders—sermons, magazine articles, and Bible study classes—telling me I should pay more attention to my wife's emotional needs. But I was in a rut so deep that I didn't even know I was in it.

It would have been much better—and easier—if I had minded the little things and not let my work, my hobbies, my friends, and our kids distract me from the only human God told me to love the way Christ loved the church. Though I've made some progress, I still have a long way to go before that deep rut is a memory.

Healthy Romance

Hopefully, we've convinced you that romancing your wife doesn't always need a payoff, and you'll be able to convince your wife that your little romantic deeds come from true-blue motives (at least most of the time). If so, here are some ideas on things you and your mate can do. While many of these suggestions may seem old hat to some couples, we've heard that one creative idea can be worth the price of a book. In an attempt to give you your money's worth, here are some surefire ways to keep the romantic flames burning.

Shopping

Go shopping with her. We know this is a brutal suggestion. It takes a brave man to walk through a mall hour after hour with no end in sight. It's clearly beyond the call of duty for most husbands.

But we found one father who actually courts his wife by "mall crawling" with her. "In a humorous way, shopping isn't a great thing for me to do, but when we do it, I say, 'man, it's nice to be by ourselves,'" says Dan.

Notes

Write notes to her. Concentrate on one area of her character that you admire, or express appreciation for what she does around the house and with the kids. Present the notes when they're least expected. (You'll be glad you did!)

Remembering to write a weekly note is nearly impossible. One father discovered that his wife is crazy about receiving little notes on a regular basis, so he devotes one hour every other month (after everyone else is in bed) to composing two-paragraph love letters. Then he doles them out week by week. He even uses different color pens so it won't look as though he wrote them all at once!

You can also turn the notes into a treasure hunt. Hide each one, giving a clue where to find the next note. The final note can tell her that she's invited out to dinner that night. (Be sure to arrange a baby sitter in advance.)

"Sacrifice what's important to you."

Small Sacrifices

Sacrifice what's important to you. Cancel that round of golf so you can watch the kids while she gets out of the house. Take the kids to the local park so she can tackle that favorite sewing project. Rent *Love Story* rather than *Rambo*. Volunteer to cook or have Domino's deliver one night a week. Carry the laundry basket down to the basement. Pick up after yourself. (Wouldn't that be a switch!) Large or small, she'll know that you're doing these things for her.

Dating

It's never too late to start dating your wife. Nearly 50 percent of the fathers who responded to our survey said they take their wives out at least once a week. (Also, 38 percent said they go out for dinner or a movie once a month, while 13 percent said it's rare for them to spend an evening together.)

After interviewing all these great dads, I (Mike) felt a tad inadequate about romancing Nicole. We've gotten into a nondating rut over the years, the biggest hindrance being a lack of finances since we've decided to make the sacrifice to keep Nicole at home with the kids. But after hearing dad after dad describe the importance of regularly dating his wife—and how much it meant to his relationship—I figured I'd better get with the program. We decided to start going out to lunch three, four times a month, and it's made a difference. The money? Well, we're just going to have to cut in other areas.

In fact, I overheard Nicole on the phone one night telling a girlfriend that she and her husband should start dating again, too. So what if you've been married fifteen years and you're on cruise control? Get out there and date!

Fathers, if you don't heed our advice, you'll regret it. "Our date night has gone by the wayside," said one father. "My wife's too tired to complain, but we both comment on how much we miss our evening together. With three young girls, we just don't have time. I do worry about getting out of balance, but the demands of work are unbelievable with the economy going the way it is. I know I'm not giving my wife enough attention."

If time is a problem, make the date a weekday lunch. "We've found Thursday lunches better than weekends because of all the activities we have going," said George.

Coffee and Conversation

Go out for food or coffee rather than a movie. The idea is to converse, and it's hard to chat in a dark multiplex with Jujubes stuck between your teeth. "If you go out for a movie," one father told us, "not much communication can go on."

Surprises

Buy her surprise gifts. Nathaniel has a good friend at a boutique, and he'll call her up and ask her to pick out an outfit or a pair of earrings since she knows his wife's size and tastes. But gifts don't have to cost much. One father, who doesn't have much money, says he buys his wife a single-stem rose for two dollars or a little card that says she's looking great. "And then you watch her glow at you," he beamed.

A Getaway

Surprise her with a nighttime or weekend getaway. Mick, from Virginia, cooked up a little surprise for his wife's birthday one year. "I took her to a fifties-type diner where the motto was 'If we can't fry it, we don't make it.' She thought it was really fun. Then I took her to the mall, peeled a fifty-dollar bill out of my wallet, and told her to go spend it."

Weekend getaways involve a bit more planning and might not be practical for a lot of couples, especially those with young children. Unless you have grandparents nearby who can take the kids for a

MEN AND ROMANCE

"It's never too late to start dating your wife."

night or two, it's a tough proposition. But it can be worked out.

Michel doesn't have parents close by, but he and his wife are friends with a young couple down the street with similar standards, ethics, and morals. Every eight weeks Michel takes his wife for a weekend get-away, and their kids stay with the neighbors. "It works out well because we take their kids when they go out of town."

Burt plans his weekend getaways a month in advance. "Recently, for our anniversary, we checked into a nice hotel in downtown San Diego, saw a play at the Old Globe theater, slept in, and went out to breakfast. We had a wonderful time."

Many downtown hotels run weekend specials to boost traffic when all the businessmen have flown home. If you live in the suburbs or a rural area, it's sometimes fun to hit the "big city."

Although I (Greg) have never done it, I've been envious of fathers who organized "total surprise" get-aways. You know, the ones where the hubby tells his wife to pack a toothbrush, some light clothes, and a smile? You don't forget weekends like that!

The Sporting Life

Get into the sporting life. One father plays social tennis with his wife every Monday night. Another goes to the driving range, where he and his wife practice their five-irons. One couple said they love to watch high school football games together. Water-skiing and snow skiing are two recreational activities that couples can do together. Tim and his wife do something most couples don't do—they fish. "That might not sound romantic, but we enjoy spending those quiet hours together," says Tim.

MEN AND ROMANCE

Say you aren't sportive? Then find a hobby you both enjoy, such as bird watching, strolling through art galleries, or gardening.

Anniversaries

Make a big deal about anniversaries. If you know what's good for you, you'll pull out all the stops for her birthday and wedding anniversaries. For Nicole's thirty-fifth birthday, I (Mike) wanted to do something *really* special. We were living in Southern California, and one morning an advertisement for the *Queen Mary* popped out in the morning newspaper. Eureka!

Thoughts of spending the night in the Queen Victoria Suite and waking up to breakfast in bed danced through my head, but we didn't have anyone to watch the kids—nor could we afford it. (Besides, her birthday fell on a school night.)

So I told Nicole to dress nicely and be prepared for *anything*. Some friends picked us up, and as we rode the sixty minutes on the L.A. freeways, I kept watching Nicole's face. She was enjoying every minute of the suspense! Once we pulled into the *Queen Mary* parking lot, we spent an afternoon tramping around the famous ocean liner. When evening fell, we topped off her birthday with the exquisite *haute cuisine* at Sir Winston's restaurant. She's still talking about that adventure.

Tom, a father from Spokane, really gets into special occasions. He and his wife celebrate their wedding anniversary *every* month—on the fifteenth! "When we first married, we got into the habit of going out on the fifteenth, our anniversary. The thing just snowballed, although it's gotten a little corny. But we still try to hold that time as important."

"If you know what's good for you, you'll pull out all the stops for her birthday and wedding anniversaries."

MEN AND ROMANCE

"Talk to Me"

If you can't go out, spend an evening talking to her. Does the TV automatically flip on each evening at your house? If it does, it's a huge communication buster. How about reserving one night each week for conversing with her? Make coffee or tea and sit in the den and look at each other and *talk*. It may seem awkward at first, but it can be the first halting step toward intimacy. One Texas father has made communication Job One. "I try to share as much as I can of what goes on during the day," he says. "Both of us try not to hold anything back, and we've practiced that since we first got married."

"What would happen in your marriage if you suddenly started treating your wife special all the time?"

Doing It All

What would happen in your marriage if you suddenly started treating your wife special all the time? At first, depending on your track record, she'll probably think you're after something. Then she'll probably ask you if something's wrong. Eventually, if you can maintain your good intentions, she'll start believing you've really changed.

Change, men. That's the point. And who can you best change? *Yourself*—not her. (You can forget about changing her anyway.) Besides, when your motives are wrong, it won't work.

When you're aboveboard, your wife's love for you will deepen. One man leaves notes on his wife's pillow ("though I'm not much of a writer"), sends her flowers occasionally, buys her inexpensive gifts, remembers special days and anniversaries, gives frequent hugs, and helps around the house. And every day he tells her he loves her—the bum!

Is he rewarded by having a warm, affectionate, attentive wife? Get this: "My reward occurs when I'm

MEN AND ROMANCE

90

doing something for her, whether she responds or not. But the biggest reward I got was when she wrote me a note that said, 'John, I feel safe with you and appreciate you because of the way you treat me. I know that when you do the little things for me you're not just trying to get sex. You really love me.' "

What hubby wouldn't love to receive a tender note such as that one?

Man to Man

1. Explore your motives for romancing your wife. Focus on motives other than physical intimacy.

2. Try to recall times when your wife has said, "I wish . . ." Now list all the endings to that construction that you can think of.

3. How can you begin to reward yourself for romancing your wife?

8

SIZZLING SEX
(We Knew That Would Get Your Attention)

Men and God's Good Gift

*Y*eh, yeh, yeh. Well, you've stuck it out so far, or maybe you flipped ahead to this chapter. That's okay. You're a red-blooded male, and we all have a passing interest in s-e-x.

In our survey, we asked our fathers: "How would you describe your sex life?" We gave them five options to check.

1. I'm very happy and satisfied.

2. It's adequate.

3. Sometimes it's good, sometimes it's not.

4. It could be better.

5. Nonexistent.

A loving doe, a graceful deer— may her breasts satisfy you always, may you ever be captivated by her love.

Proverbs

And the results were:

- 51 percent "very happy and satisfied"
- 18 percent "it's adequate"
- 15 percent "sometimes it's good, sometimes it's not"
- 15 percent "it could be better"
- 1 percent "it's nonexistent"

93

We've got some pretty happy and satisfied guys out there. The overwhelming majority said *no problemo*. And that's great, since that's how God planned it. Sex was His idea; it was created by Him, and it was intended for our pleasure within the bonds of marriage.

Call a Sexpert

But sexually satisfied men aren't the norm, according to the findings of psychologist Jonathan Kramer and his wife, Diane Dunaway, *Why Men Don't Get Enough Sex and Women Don't Get Enough Love*. Based on their research, 55 percent of men said they are unhappy with their sex lives. (And nearly two-thirds of all women said they are dissatisfied with the amount of love they receive from their husbands.)

What gives, guys?

Our hunch—and it's only a hunch, since we're not "sexperts"—is that Christian men, living in a solid marriage relationship, experience more sexual satisfaction than the general population. (Remember, we interviewed dads recommended by their church pastors and members of the Focus on the Family public affairs staff.)

These are men who understand that you can't turn off the lights and expect sexual favors. "Your wife wants to get to know you," explained Jim, who added that one thing he's learned as a husband is that romance still counts. "You can't expect your wife to hop into bed at your pleasure and think things will happen. It's important to make sure she feels loved, not used. To do that you have to be a helpmate. You have to have an ongoing relationship during the day by not taking her for granted. When I clean up after dinner, that shows I love her because she knows I

> *"Our hunch—and it's only a hunch, since we're not 'sexperts'—is that Christian men, living in a solid marriage relationship, experience more sexual satisfaction than the general population."*

94

hate rinsing dishes and washing pots and pans. For me and my wife, sex *does* begin in the kitchen."

Another father said, "If you're *demanding* something from your wife, then it can't be an open and caring relationship. I think of that scripture, 'Husbands, love your wives as Christ loves the church.' That's not demanding love. Before I realized that, I was trying to get something for myself, instead of being able to enjoy her for who she is."

One honest guy confessed, "The first three or four years of marriage, I'm sure my wife felt like her job was to service the 'big stud.' While I'll still manipulate the situation and wish she would come through sexually more often, I've gotten over the stage of 'punishing' her—by pulling away—or indirectly punishing me—by masturbating in the next twenty-four hours.

"The strong move for me is to roll back over, grab her hand, and admit that the things I did weren't loving. It's a struggle to show love to her when she says no. But as our love grows, it does get easier."

Another father said one thing he and his wife do is make sure she orgasms first. "With that comes an attitude that I'm not just doing this for myself. I want her to enjoy this the most so her needs will be met. It gets back to honoring her and placing her needs above my own."

Master the Motive

The absolute—bottom line—key that unlocks our sex lives is our motives. In *What Wives Wish Their Husbands Knew About Women*, Dr. Dobson stresses nine common motives that aren't always so pure:

1. Sex is often permitted as a marital duty.

2. It is offered to repay or secure a favor.

3. It represents conquest or victory.

MEN AND GOD'S GOOD GIFT

"The absolute—bottom line—key that unlocks our sex lives is our motives."

4. It stands as a substitute for verbal communication.

5. It is used to overcome feelings of inferiority (especially in men who seek proof of their masculinity).

6. It is an enticement for emotional love (especially by women who use their bodies to obtain masculine attention).

7. It is a defense against anxiety and tension.

8. It is provided or withheld in order to manipulate the partner.

9. It is engaged in for the purpose of bragging to others.

Dr. Dobson adds that these "non-loving" reasons for participating in the sex act rob it of meaning and reduce it to an empty and frustrating social game. "Sexual intercourse in marriage should bring pleasure, of course, but it should also provide a method of communicating a very deep spiritual commitment. Women are much more sensitive to this need," he says (from Dr. James Dobson, *What Wives Wish Their Husbands Knew About Women*, Tyndale House Publishers, 1975, used by permission).

Unless motives are identified and dealt with by both partners, selfishness and resentment will multiply as the years pass by. Recognizing them (with yourself), admitting them (to your wife), and making honest attempts at solving selfish motives (with God's help) will foster a level of trust that marriages need for long-term health.

All You Need Is Love

The sexual revolution, glamorized by such groups as the Beatles in the sixties, has taken its toll. For those

MEN AND GOD'S GOOD GIFT

caught up in "free love" during their pre-Christian days, the cost of sin can reach out over decades.

One dad, who fooled around before marriage, confessed that his present-day sex life wasn't so hot. *What goes around comes around,* and it's a result, he feels, of having disobeyed God's immutable laws. Lately his sex life is improving, but only because he's made an effort to romance his wife. "Without that foundation, sparks aren't going to fly," he said.

Another father told us that one lesson you definitely want to learn before marriage is self-control. "In our courting days, we did everything but—. We'd get to a point; then we'd stop. That went on for over a year. After marriage, her body was programmed to stop, even though we didn't have to. We struggled sexually for years. I really believe the reason we struggled was because we didn't develop self-control. That's one bad thing about being young and in love; you can't see the whole picture."

Bill told us that prior to becoming a Christian, he was demanding and selfish. "I didn't consider my wife's needs. I think once we both came to the Lord and got some teaching, we relaxed and learned to give and take. I would say that sex, like the rest of our relationship, has gotten better and better over time," says Bill.

Those who waited until marriage—and they deserve a twenty-one-gun salute—say that waiting was the right thing. "We have a real healthy marriage," said one father, "and we both were inexperienced. But we learned together. I know not everyone can say that, but it made a difference with us."

Comic Relief

Before we go too much further, let's take a laugh break.

The Top Ten Reasons
Not To Have Sex Tonight

10 If your wife becomes pregnant, you'll have to listen to her bellyache for the next nine months.

9 There's no such thing as "safe sex."

8 If you can't afford another kid right now, why take a chance?

7 The Lord could return at *any* moment.

6 You're all out of shaving cream.

5 The phone might ring, and someone could ask what you were doing.

4 The box spring is too squeaky and the headboard is too loose.

3 You could have a heart attack and die.

2 You might not finish during the commercial break.

1 Your kids might walk in on you.

Some of those reasons aren't that funny. In fact, more than a few fathers mentioned that having kids in the vicinity threw a wet blanket, so to speak, over their love life.

"It's difficult with two kids across the hall," said one father. "We're not sure if we're going to wake them up, so that can inhibit things."

"It seems as though there's always somebody in the house," complained another dad, referring to times when the neighbor kids stay for a sleepover.

The old-fashioned bolt on the door can help. "We have a lock on our door, and that gives my wife

"More than a few fathers mentioned that having kids in the vicinity threw a wet blanket, so to speak, over their love life."

MEN AND GOD'S GOOD GIFT

security," said one father. "My folks had one, and I knew when it was locked not to go in there."

But another father said a lock doesn't do him any good. "When we turn the lock, the kids come and cry and kick the door."

How do some fathers spice up their sex lives? One man said—get this—that each spring under the guise of pretending to produce another child, he and his wife have sex every night for six weeks! Forty-two straight nights is a couple of years' worth for most guys. We were so stunned by this revelation that we forgot to ask him whose idea it was or how she agreed to it.

Other fathers said weekend getaways twice a year were a great way to break out of the Saturday-night doldrums. Something about new surroundings and a respite from the kids was enough to energize tired parents. "We're in our middle thirties," says John, "and at this stage, I think most men would say 'Well, it could be better' for the simple reason that when one parent isn't tired, the other is."

Another dad told us he has friends who let him use a townhouse forty miles south of the Mexican border. "The last time we went down alone, we ate lobster and *carne asada* for two nights, walked on the beach, made love, did all the good things. We had time to read . . . and talk to each other. What's nice about going away to an isolated place is that there isn't a whole lot to do," he said.

Expectations Unfulfilled

Before Jay married, he used to pray for a Christian nymphomaniac. "Just joking!" he quickly added.

Actually, what he really wanted in a wife was a godly Marilyn Monroe. (This Jay really has a sense of humor.) In a case of life imitating art, Jay thought he'd move things along by buying his wife a sexy black negligée for Christmas. We're talking *hot*.

"What's that?" she screamed when she took it out of the box. Jay learned real quick that black negligées

What Are the Top Five Reasons Why the Wife Should Initiate Sex More Often?

5 It will get rid of her headache.

4 She won't have to see her husband de-meaning himself by begging for it all the time.

3 She'll feel less guilty when she goes to the mall.

2 It will help convince hubby he's still a major stud-muffin (even if he really isn't).

1 The exercise will help thin her thighs.

What Are The Top Eight Reasons She Doesn't Initiate Sex More Often?

8 It isn't Saturday night.

7 She prefers to let him make the first move so she can be assured that he can still speak.

6 It's better to let a sleeping dog lie.

5 Her negligées are at the cleaners.

4 It would only encourage him.

3 He refuses to turn off the TV set.

2 He insists on keeping his socks on.

1 His idea of foreplay is yelling, "Yo, hon!"

MEN AND GOD'S GOOD GIFT

were not her bag. He can laugh about it now. "When you first get married, you're trying to figure out who your spouse is. After she told me she didn't like the black negligée, I could have gotten angry with her and built a wall around myself. But I decided that if I am thinking negative thoughts, those thoughts are not coming from the Lord, but from Satan, who wants to drive a wedge between us. I need to focus on the good things. It keeps my love fresh. Today we are more crazy about each other than ever before, and we've been married twenty years."

Sexual Stupidity

Have you listened when a good friend tells you what *not* to do? Well, listen up. The following suggestions were mentioned most when we asked fathers what their wives considered a turnoff.

- *Sexual innuendos.* We convince our wives that we have one-track minds by the small asides we make ("Feeling hot, honey?"). You may not think you're getting through, but she's getting the message loud and clear. *You can sleep on your side of the bed tonight, buster.*
- *Touching and grabbing.* Another sexually stupid thing is to think a well-placed pinch will do something for her. All this does is tell her you're horny.
- *Misreading the signals.* Not every cuddle or hug between the two of you will lead to sex. Even if making love happens less frequently than you'd like, fight the urge to take physical contact to the next level every time.
- *Assuming she's like you.* "I didn't have much of a clue how to meet my wife's sexual needs," said one father. "I assumed that since I wanted sex,

she did too. But it doesn't work that way. We joke about it now because I finally realized that sex begins hours before it happens."

- *Not talking before and after*. The best way to convince the wife your intentions are on the up and up is to treat her like an intimate companion. "My wife always knows what I'm really after by how much time I spend talking to her before and cuddling afterward," says Kurt. "If I roll over, she feels used. She'll be less likely to respond the next time."

- *Impatience*. When you're newly married, you probably haven't gotten the hang of arousing your wife. You tend to think the act itself is the ticket. So instead of waiting until she's really ready, you move too fast. Again, this communicates selfishness and makes your wife feel used.

Once sexual habits are formed, even if they're formed in ignorance, it takes a long time to convince her that you want to be a patient, attentive lover. Remember, too, that building her self-image and appropriately romancing her are all part of the mix. Be gentle. Stroke her hair and give her a back rub (that will slow things down!).

Your wife will be convinced of your intentions when you demonstrate patience, courtesy, and respect over the long haul. While starting over (in other words, retraining yourself) seems like an arduous process (and it just might be), the long-term health of the marriage may be at stake.

When you hit your mid-thirties after a few years of marriage, you'll want genuine intimacy more than sexual release, something your wife has probably longed for from the start. She's probably been waiting for you to catch on!

> *"Once sexual habits are formed, even if they're formed in ignorance, it takes a long time to convince her that you want to be a patient, attentive lover."*

MEN AND GOD'S GOOD GIFT

Starting Over

Perhaps the toughest thing you can do with your wife is to admit your past mistakes and promise to start fresh, especially in the areas of romance and sex. Unfortunately, many men figure it's too late to change and not worth the hassle. That's tragic thinking.

Even though your wife may not respond the way you want, you must make an effort to bridge the sexual gap. Unfortunately, there isn't a simple strategy for healing the intimacy between you and your wife. But here are a few suggestions to get you started:

1. Make a list of dumb things you've done in the past. Write down things your wife has mentioned that bother her. Go through the list and vow to quit doing the stupid stuff.

2. Confess your selfishness to God. Ask Him to help you overcome the patterns that have been set. If you have any hidden sins to confess, do it. God knows about them, and He also knows that the only way to deal with dark closets is to shed light in them. If problems are deep-seated, then a pastor, counselor, or trusted friend could give you the guidance you need.

3. If there are deep scars or little intimate contact between you and your wife, ask her for forgiveness as well. Don't make any promises about "everything's going to be different." Just tell her you're motivated to change. Seek her prayers and give her permission to gently point out your selfishness.

4. Realize that it may take months to convince her that you're sincere about changing. If you've manipulated your sexual relationship to satisfy your needs without a concern for hers, then you've broken her trust.

"Do not—repeat, do not—expect her to respond overnight to the 'new you.' She'll need time to judge whether your changes are for real."

5. Practice caring behaviors that show her you're making an effort. Do not—repeat, *do not*—expect her to respond overnight to the "new you." She'll need time to judge whether your changes are for real.

6. Make sure your motives aren't to get more sex. She'll see through that in no time. Then you'll have to start all over again, but this time your motives will be even more suspect.

7. Treat her like a cherished treasure, without expecting anything in return. This is where it will get *very* difficult. We're such selfish creatures that to cuddle and caress our wives without expecting anything in return goes against our grain.

What About Your Needs?

The goal in changing your sexual tune is to seek a level of intimacy you've never known before. Once you're approaching it, you'll be able to talk openly with your wife.

One husband told us how far he's come in this area: "We finally reached a point where I could talk about what goes on inside me sexually. I've always been very aware of my own personal cycle as a man. I know that my thoughts stay pure about three to five days after having sex with my wife. Since it's rare that a women's drive is anywhere close to that number of days, we'd often go weeks between sex. It was frustrating!

"In the old days, about the fifth day, I'd start doing all sorts of stuff to get my wife to meet my needs. Subtle things that to her were never that subtle. Now, because I've made a commitment to do things better, I don't have to. We talked about what is reasonable to her—and to me. It's brought both of us balance and harmony. I was able to explain that when we don't have sex it creates tension. Sharing has made me more vulnerable, but manipulation is what wives fear most, especially sexual manipulation. No one likes to feel used. But I was able to share with her that I'm totally dependent on her. 'There's something you have, and you're the only one who has it.' I could go out and get it some other way, but I'm a Christian, and that would really be bad news for me to even think in that direction.

"Because my wife was able to see that I was being honest, she didn't sense I was trying to manipulate her. She never said I don't believe you. She trusted me."

Courageous Patience

The lifelong process toward intimate relations with your wife, which may include sexual fulfillment, begins with honest communication.

Men can't ignore the sexual pressure, nor can we go searching for fulfillment elsewhere: either with our minds (which we'll talk about in the next chapter) or with someone else. Both avenues are spiritually destructive, not only to our marriage and our children, but also to the watching world. We pray that you will never succumb to those temptations. Instead, seek sexual satisfaction only from your wife, and you'll be well on the road to *real* intimacy.

Man to Man

1. How do you rank your own sex life on the scale given at the beginning of this chapter?

"The lifelong process toward intimate relations with your wife, which may include sexual fulfillment, begins with honest communication."

2. To what extent can you and your wife discuss the satisfactions and the longings of your sexual relationship?

3. How can you go about establishing a more satisfying balance in this area?

MEN AND GOD'S GOOD GIFT

9

WHEN YOU'RE DYING FOR A SIP

Men and Their Minds

We can't talk about maximizing those most important hours of the day without tackling the toughest part—keeping our minds free from distractions (you know which ones we mean) so we can think of others first. If any chapter needed a Top Ten list, this one's it.

The Top Ten Ways That Never Work to Clean Up Your Mind?

Who can say, "I have kept my heart pure; I am clean and without sin"?
Proverbs

10 Have your wife rip out the lingerie ads from all the department store catalogs before you see them.

9 Stay out of restaurants where all the waitresses are under twenty-five.

8 Record all sporting events so you can fast-forward through the Swedish bikini team beer commercials.

7 Spend a summer day relaxing at the beach or at the local pool.

6 Rent R-rated movies with the intent to fast-forward through the "hot parts."

5 Only read books that are on the *New York Times* best-seller list.

4 Watch network sitcoms instead of the Bravo channel.

3 Try to think about other things when the guys at work tell raunchy jokes.

2 Read *Playboy* just for the articles.

1 Go to PG-13 movies instead of R-rated ones.

When I (Greg) lived in Seattle, I met with my pastor every other week. He was—and remains to this day—one of the most godly, committed Christians I know. He's married to a beautiful wife, and his kids are all tracking for the Lord. God is multiplying his ministry each year.

Once I asked him a question that had been bothering me for a long time.

"Lately, Bill, I've been struggling with my thought life—you know, thinking about things I shouldn't. When will I grow out of it?"

I was in my early thirties at the time, and he was forty-something. I thought he must have a quick answer, a snappy solution.

He looked at me and without hesitating said, "You won't."

That wasn't the response I expected to hear. I wanted my friend to say something along the lines of

- "If you memorize these ten verses, your mind will be as pure as the driven snow."

- "I know this book on spiritual discipline that's just the ticket. I'm sure it will help you as much as it helped me."

MEN AND THEIR MINDS

- "As soon as you hit your forties, you won't think about those things as often. It'll go away. Just relax."

- "You'd better get yourself a men's accountability group, where you'll be asked tough questions about your impure thought life."

- "The Holy Spirit can cleanse your mind if only you have enough faith and believe in His power."

No such luck.

Instead, all I heard was "You won't."

Bill was right, of course. You can't turn a street corner or flip on a TV without running up against a provocatively dressed young woman. Billboards portray larger-than-life blondes draped across car hoods trying to convince us that one comes with the other. The beer-and-bikini TV ads don't satisfy your taste for a brewski, either. Sex sells, and boy, society is giving us the hard pitch.

Where Does It Start?

Several men we talked with admitted the struggle started long ago. One man remembers his sister's boyfriend bringing over a box of hard-core pornographic magazines. He had just turned thirteen. The magazines opened him up to a world he had never seen before. "Just as my hormones were kicking in, I was given easy access to stuff I was really curious about. It was easy to OD on the stuff."

Throughout his teenage years, his hunger for skin magazines never abated. "You feed your mind enough of that stuff and the images become impossible to erase. Even after I became a Christian, the desire to look at naked women didn't quit. I thought it would go away after I got married in my early twenties. Unfortunately, I couldn't rid my mind of what I'd pro-

"Even after I became a Christian, the desire to look at naked women didn't quit."

grammed it to 'enjoy.' It was illicit and addictive. I always felt like I was getting away with something, especially after I married."

Sometimes he got his problem under control. Months would pass and then—in a moment of weakness—he'd succumb again.

His story is more common than we would like to admit. Some of us grew up in "enlightened" homes where *Penthouse* was regular coffee-table fare. Or we went to schools where buddies kept a copy of *Hustler* stuffed in their locker.

Years later pictures of naked women can resurrect themselves in our minds. We end up doing the very things we hate, and guilt paralyzes our ability to think that God can use—or even love—us.

Satan has laid a clever trap. Think about it. He handcuffs our ability to lead by making us think that God didn't face what we face; that He can't love men who've fed themselves a steady diet of porn.

The Bible, however, states that God knows exactly what men go through. Hebrews 4:15–16 makes this perfectly clear: "For we do not have a high priest who is unable to sympathize with our weaknesses, but we have one who has been tempted in every way, just as we are—yet was without sin." The next verse supplies the hope that men need if we are to continue pursuing God and a clear conscience: "Let us then approach the throne of grace with confidence, so that we may receive mercy and find grace to help us in our time of need."

With that type of invitation, no man should resist coming to Jesus, wayward mind or not. He will help us—if we let Him.

Tearing out the Roots

What usually submarines men who dabble past the adolescent stage of sexual curiosity is a feeding frenzy of impure thoughts. Alcoholics Anonymous would call it sipping. We can sip, too, when it comes to looking at the ladies. It might be a bit-too-long stare at a buxom woman's low-cut blouse or getting an eyeful of the latest "thong" bathing suit. Believing that "a little bit won't hurt" is what keeps impure thoughts bouncing around the brain—and keeps men in bondage.

Even though the siren call is strong, Satan does not force us to follow through on the temptation. However helpless we may feel to fight the call, we make the choices: "When tempted, no one should say, 'God is tempting me.' For God cannot be tempted by evil, nor does he tempt anyone; but each one is tempted when, by his own evil desire, he is dragged away and enticed. Then, after desire has conceived, it gives birth to sin; and sin, when it is fullgrown, gives birth to death" (James 1:13–15).

Temptation, remember, is not a sin. It's the acting upon it that gets us in trouble.

What Can Be Done?

Each man is different. Some of us are sent into overload by walking past a "Frederick's of Hollywood" store at the local mall. For others, all it takes is an accidental brush with soft-core porn—*Sports Illustrated's* famous swimsuit issue, to name a well-known example.

Others find their minds clear for a few days after having sex with their wives, while some feel they have to take their sex life into their own hands in order to rid themselves of uninvited thoughts. For many, it's extremely discouraging: *Why do I keep falling into the same pit?*

One key to winning the battle is to decrease the opportunities to sip. Believe us, it takes a healthy dose

"Believing that 'a little bit won't hurt' is what keeps impure thoughts bouncing around the brain—and keeps men in bondage."

of discipline and determination. The secret for the Apostle Paul was taking "captive every thought to make it obedient to Christ" (2 Corinthians 10:5). That's a pretty good strategy to follow.

If you're going to whip the problem, you're going to have to practice avoidance. In other words:

- Don't drive by stores that carry pornography.
- Use the channel flicker if TV shows or commercials are too suggestive or show too much skin.
- Listen to Christian music instead of a secular station. Old songs can trigger memories of what you were doing in the "good ol' days." If you don't have a Christian radio station in your area, purchase Christian music or a series of messages from a speaker you enjoy. Or you can tape Scripture passages to the dashboard and memorize them during your commute time.

Things You Can Do

Our surveys and interviews provided a number of other ways to corral a wandering mind and any actions it could lead to. Here's the list:

- Do all you can to remain in an intimate relationship with your wife.
- If you blame your wife for your lack of self-control, remember, too, that every woman has faults. You made a marriage commitment that you need to keep.
- Remember that lust saddens our heavenly Father.
- Avoid situations that stimulate impure thoughts. When under stress, pressure, or anger, use Philippians 4:8–9: "Finally, brothers, whatever is true, whatever is noble, whatever is right, whatever is pure, whatever is lovely, whatever is admirable—if anything is excellent or praiseworthy—think about such things."

MEN AND THEIR MINDS

- Know your human tendencies. Shut down a lustful thought before it takes root. Switch to thoughts of how beautiful your wife is.

- Practice not staring at anything that pushes your hot button.

- Think of your wife and kids and weigh the consequences of being caught.

- When it's appropriate, talk to your wife about some of the causes.

- Imagine how you'd feel if your wife did the same thing.

- Understand that if you pursue lustful thoughts, then you're hurting yourself, God, and your family.

- When you're most vulnerable, confide in a good friend. Ask him to pray for you. Ask him for suggestions to keep you out of trouble.

- If the problem does not abate, seek professional counseling or talk to your pastor.

In reality, life doesn't offer pat answers, but this statement is true: We are who we are when we're by ourselves.

Our thought life is something only *we* can decide to work on. Most men agree it's a lifelong battle. It's a struggle that robs us of the integrity we need and the inner purity we really want. But it doesn't have to make us ineffective husbands and fathers.

If we allow it, God can even use our past "failures" to bring about His redemptive work. When Paul described his struggle in Romans 7, he came to this conclusion: "What a wretched man I am! Who will rescue me from this body of death? Thanks be to God—through Jesus Christ our Lord! (vv. 24–25).

Admitting failure is tough for men. Recognizing that we're captive to sexy thoughts should force us to our knees. If we can recognize our weakness, then we can also help others overcome theirs. That may be *the* most masculine and courageous thing we can do.

"Our thought life is something only we can decide to work on. Most men agree it's a lifelong battle."

For who can say, "I have kept my heart pure; I am clean and without sin"? (Proverbs 20:9). Instead, we should guard our hearts, for they are "the wellspring of life" (Proverbs 4:23).

Man to Man

1. What situations represent the greatest danger to the purity of your thought life?

2. List some methods you have used to drive out impure thoughts. Can you add any new ones from this chapter?

3. Don't stop at the obvious answer as you think about ways your wife can help you with this issue.

MEN AND THEIR MINDS

10

LET'S KEEP IT PROFESSIONAL

Men and Their Friends

Whether we wear a white or blue collar to work, many of us keep our colleagues at arm's length. One reason is that we have so little time. If we do manage to unloose a few hours of freedom, we usually invest it in our families or ourselves.

- I have my territory, you have yours. Let's not get in each other's way.
- I can't act vulnerable, or I might reveal one of my weaknesses.
- I have my pride to maintain. Besides, I'm more insecure than I look.
- I'm in a hurry; I don't have time for friendships.

That's life in the big city these days. Too many plates are spinning in the air, which is why we're constantly looking for shortcuts—even with friendships. We don't have time to scratch beneath the surface, so we make an unconscious choice to keep our friendships on a professional level.

We don't let people see behind the mask.

We're rather good at it, aren't we? Why not? We've been practicing it for years. "Don't let anyone get too close." "Keep up the facade." "Act tough." "Don't ever let them see you sweat."

As iron sharpens iron, so one man sharpens another.

A man of many companions may come to ruin, but there is a friend who sticks closer than a brother.

He who walks with the wise grows wise, but a companion of fools suffers harm.
Proverbs

115

The process starts at an early age. A Washington state pastor admitted: "We've taught people early on *not* to admit they have struggles. Do you know how we did it? By being judgmental if they confess one. We've sealed men up in their sins."

Too true. For example, what happens when a child admits a mistake and then is punished right on the spot? The child learns a lesson all right: next time he won't 'fess up, nor will he be honest about future mistakes. It's safer that way.

In the same way, if we don't come clean about our hidden life, we avoid punishment, embarrassment, or a shot to the pride by programming our brains for surface professional relationships, especially with other men.

It works too. No one really knows us.

But at what cost?

The biggest price we pay is this: closets in our life go unopened—struggles such as

- emotional childhood scars
- a thought-life careening out of control
- bitterness toward your spouse
- unmet physical needs
- an inability to be genuine with your kids
- bouts of anger that only your family witnesses
- hidden addictions to pornography, sexual immorality, and drugs—and the guilt that goes along with them

Can you imagine the deep remorse of one father who admitted he made his wife have an abortion so his career "wouldn't be held back"? Though he's repented and gotten it off his chest, he'll carry that pain for the rest of his life.

Without genuine male friendships, we're apt to leave closets unopened, closets that need to have some light shed into them. Sadly, we live under an

MEN AND THEIR FRIENDS

unwritten rule that says, "I'm okay, you're okay. And if you're not okay, don't tell anyone."

Write a New Rule

Howard Hendricks, professor emeritus at the Dallas Theological Seminary, once said, "A man who is not in a group with other men is an accident waiting to happen."

Some of the fathers we interviewed were candidates for 911. While 51 percent said they were in a weekly Bible study, only 45 percent were involved in a group with other men that offered accountability and encouragement. And that's probably a high figure compared to the general Christian population.

If you don't want to wake up to a marriage or a faith that has self-destructed, then you'll have to convince yourself of a new rule: "I'm not okay, you're not okay. And if we can both admit it, we can do something about it."

How?

Very few of us could ever manage the courage to open all our closet doors at once. Perhaps you swung one open before, but you were judged cruelly. Admittedly, risks are involved, risks that seem too high. But we have to take chances, men, if we want peace with God. Then we can *really* expect God to use us in our families, our neighborhood, or our church.

An Illinois church elder has heard men describe everything from deep-seated hate for their fathers to extramarital affairs. He's convinced that admitting dark struggles, at appropriate times to people who can encourage and help, promotes healing and forgiveness.

"Sin isn't something we've goofed up and moved into," says the elder. "It's not our specific sins that are the problem. It's our condition that's passed down

MEN AND THEIR FRIENDS

"Without genuine male friendships, we're apt to leave closets unopened, closets that need to have some light shed into them."

117

from generation to generation. It has to be dealt with by Christ. The only way to do that is bring sin into the light and allow Him to use other men—with a similar sin nature—to minister grace, forgiveness, and hope. They have to be reminded that God hasn't abandoned them."

Finding another man or a group of men to confide in isn't an easy assignment, nor can it be solved overnight. Meeting up with even *one* other man who has the maturity to accept us, dark closets and all, takes diligence. We talked to several men on this subject.

Andrew agreed he should seek out more male friendships. "But I don't make friends very easily," he says. "I grew up close to my mother's family, and they were nearly all females. That has made it tough for me to open up to other men."

Frank tried to find accountability through a Bible study group at his church, but the friendships he made were superficial. "I'd love to have an accountability-type relationship with some of the men, but I haven't made the match I feel is necessary."

For Frank, it's simply a matter of time before God leads the right men his way. And since he mentioned the word *accountability*, let's spend a few minutes on that subject.

For many men, the word *accountability* conjures up the fearful feeling of having to tell secrets about yourself, secrets you don't want anyone else to know. Some may think, *What if it ever gets out that I've been in one of those adult bookstores or massage parlors? The whole church would know. My life and marriage would be ruined.*

Accountability can be a scary word. But really, no one can make you share something you don't want to share. If someone is in that deep (and Christian men have been known to be!), and he can't trust the group or the guy, he'll simply beat around the bush or keep his mouth shut.

> "Meeting up with even one other man who has the maturity to accept us, dark closets and all, takes diligence."

MEN AND THEIR FRIENDS

What should you do? The first step is simply finding one man (or several men) with whom you feel comfortable. Find someone with whom you have good rapport, a man who can sharpen—and accept—you no matter what. A good friend.

Once a friend invited Don, a New Jersey businessman, to a men's retreat. Don spent the weekend talking about his difficulties being a father, son, and husband. "It was nice to be able to share those things," he says. "As a result, I have become more and more convinced that men need a safe place to talk with other men."

The momentum of Don's weekend retreat has continued right into his weekly accountability meetings. "The group I got into was very casual, but just recently it's been getting a little more open," he says. "The leadership is informal, and the guys can share as deeply as they feel comfortable. We started out with people talking about their backgrounds, which was very interesting. I knew these people from church. But I never really *knew* them. Learning how they were raised, what hurts they experienced growing up, who their models were, and how they raise their kids has helped me understand who they are today."

Don's on the right path.

Another father told us he's in a "minor league elder-type group. The church is grooming us for future leadership," says Robert. "It's very personal, and we do share our hurts. One guy lost his job, but because he had the support of the group, he said it was the best year of his life.

"This group has one drawback: it's too large. But that hasn't stopped me. There's one other guy in my same life circumstances that I've clicked with. We've been able to peel that extra layer away and really be personal with each other."

When we interviewed Billy Joe, it was all he could do to contain his enthusiasm. "I'm in a group right now that's really working," he said. "We're able to hold each other to goals and spiritual disciplines we've said we wanted to work toward."

Those ideals were put to the test once when the group took a couple of months off. None of the fathers was able to stay consistently in the Word. "One man walked out on his wife," recalled Billy Joe. "When we finally reorganized, we were able to bring him back. Without this group, his marriage would now be finished, and his kids probably scarred for life."

Closets will be opened by caring, nonjudgmental groups. It takes time, but who wouldn't say it's worth the wait?

Heard a Good One Lately?

Have you ever asked a friend or acquaintance to join an accountability group but were turned down? If you have, perhaps you've heard one of these excuses.

The Wrong Type

"I can't find the right type of friends."

Baloney. Every church has a breakfast group of some sort. While the fellowship is great, it usually scratches the surface. Most breakfast groups rarely foster an atmosphere where men can open dark closets. Instead, look at them as a good place to start forming friendships. You'll need to keep an eye peeled for men you'll click with—and who've shown a measure of honesty.

Lack of Expertise

"Guys my age don't have any answers."

Eddie, from Orlando, says accountability groups at his church are too age-specific. "I have a tough time relating to men who can't see the forest for the trees. We're all going through similar struggles, but there don't seem to be any answers. Personally, I'd rather spend my time with older men who've been around the block. I know about six older guys whom I can call right now to talk about anything."

Eddie makes a good point. It's hard to yank yourself out of the mud if those helping you are in the thick of it with you. But Eddie's on shaky ground for a couple of reasons.

First, unless we're in a regular group where the tough questions are being asked on a consistent basis, we'll have a tendency to keep things hidden. Satan is very crafty when it comes to our closets. He knows those hidden things keep us ineffective as believers, husbands, and fathers. Because it's risky to admit struggles, we need face-to-face reminders of unconditional love from brothers—at least every other week—in order to feel it's safe enough to share. If not, the walls go right up to the ceiling.

Second, older men in the faith may have tons of wisdom to draw on, but for the most part, they weren't "trained" to be genuine. Many have simply lived for too long under the male standard of keeping relationships on the surface. If they have learned the art of getting beneath the surface, the issues they face today aren't at all like the ones men in their twenties and thirties are experiencing.

Most of the guys we talked with told us God was watching over their accountability groups carefully. "He's never allowed all four of us to be down for the count at the same time," said Dean. "Someone's always been outside the forest to offer encouragement and hope."

Too Little Time

"Who's got the time?"

"It's hard to yank yourself out of the mud if those helping you are in the thick of it with you."

Dale has tried to initiate an accountability group with other men, but all he gets is a polite brushoff. "It seems as though no one's got the time. I'd still like to find that one guy I could bare my soul to and not be rejected," says Dale.

Genuine friendships that care enough to go the extra mile—and stick around an extra hour—are, unfortunately, all too rare. We're busy, or perhaps we're "satisfied" with the way things are going. We might be sailing through life, and there doesn't appear to be a storm from here all the way to the International Date Line. So we don't feel we have a need.

When we brought up this subject in our interviews, we learned that waiting until the mid-thirties or mid-forties to develop close relationships usually meant they weren't going to happen. Most men wished they had gotten into the habit of opening closets earlier in life.

Don't give up hope though. Dozens of men are in the same boat as you, and they're probably dying for more than surface fellowship with other guys. Be diligent, and you'll find one.

Too Little Patience

"It takes too long to get to a deeper level."

Ten years ago, Caleb started a Bible study every Tuesday from 6:00 to 7:30 A.M. The group was comprised of a cross-section of guys in their early thirties. At the outset, however, none of the men were about to discuss the big issues of life. After a while, their wives decided they'd get together once a month and pray for the group.

Within months the men began to make a breakthrough. They opened up and really started sharing. Their love for each other turned a big corner as they realized they were all going through similar struggles. "Finally, a couple of the guys and I got to another

MEN AND THEIR FRIENDS

level," said Caleb. "I don't think it could have happened without our wives praying and the older guys in the group. They provided good mentoring."

Too Mature

"I'm a more mature Christian than other men I know."

"Unfortunately," says Pete, "the friends I've made at church see me more as a counselor. I'm a little older in Christ, so some of the men look up to me. Yet I know I'm at my most dangerous point when I think it's safe."

Finding other men with the same level of maturity is not easy. The expectation of "perfection" makes it tougher to reach out. Ministers told us they particularly struggle with this. "How do you admit weaknesses when everyone looks to you as the model?" asked one pastor. The answer may be to seek out other pastors in similar situations. Yes, it's potentially threatening, but *every* man has closets to open.

Already Accountable

"I'm already accountable to my family."

"I used to be in an accountability group," says Clifford, "and for some it works great. But I've got a wife and three kids who keep me accountable. We're real open with each other, and we're each other's best friends. It's just not a need in my life."

Though this type of situation is rare, it can occur. To say that a group of men is needed for every man sounds legalistic.

We see a red flag, however, and it's knowing the nature of men. Our habit of hiding parts of our lives is so ingrained that it would be easy to rationalize away our need for being asked the tough questions by men who care.

Is your relationship with your wife close enough for you to share these thoughts?

- Honey, there's a new secretary in the office who's flirting with the guys. Pray for me, and ask me how I'm doing every week.
- I'm just not motivated to spend time with God.
- I resent you for paying more attention to the kids than to me.

Loss

"I had a good friend once, but now things have changed."

Jacob started jogging with another guy at noon at a nearby YMCA. Over a period of two years, they built a foundation of mutual trust and often shared concerns with each other. One day, they felt the freedom to talk about deeper doubts and struggles. "It was great to finally get it out," said Jacob, "but unfortunately, our business commitments took us in different directions. I still haven't found anyone to take his place."

If you've ever had someone close enough to be real with (and you know how long it takes to build trust), you know how draining it can be just thinking about starting over. But we must.

I (Greg) understand my need to be an open book with at least one other man. Over the last ten years, I've lived in four different cities, and each time, I've had to initiate new friendships. To speed along the process I go through several steps:

1. I recognize the fact that if I keep my life hidden, I'm setting myself up for big-time problems.

2. I ask God to show me at least one guy I can start meeting with to test the waters. (I've found that starting a group with three or more other men is the best route. That way, if one has to leave, I don't have to start over again.) Because God knows my needs, He's been faithful to point me to the right men.

3. Once I find several men interested in a group, we start meeting weekly. Lunchtime has always worked best for us.

4. Finally, after about nine months of meeting together, it may be time to open a closet. In my last group, I was the first to test the waters. To be honest, if someone hadn't done something soon, the group might have died. But once we opened up, our relationships rocketed to a whole new level.

Not a Magic Word

Here are some quotations from some of the fathers we interviewed:

> When I'm in a group, I examine myself more often and I realize I'm not in this life alone. It's really kept me from having to play the game of perfection.

> I call mine a "men's group." Accountability smacks of another performance model I have to live up to. I'm tired of performing. The last thing I want in my group is to reinforce that value.

> We don't go down a list to ask what we did that was a crime, but through the process of just being honest, things come out. We talk. Some guys are flat-out struggling with terrible sins. It often takes six to seven weeks before they can get up the courage to even hint at a problem. Going down a list would just encourage a guy to lie. If he lies for eight weeks, he's not going to be honest the ninth week either.

Every group and relationship is different. There's a process God is orchestrating for each of us to address the dark closets that need His touch. To say there is a "right" way to open up the closets in your life would be untrue. One fact, however, remains obvious: The unexamined life never gets to the questions of what God wants us to do.

Coming face to face with ourselves by meeting with other men who are going through the same issues is a tool God uses to get us to shed light on the darkness our sin nature loves to hide. We know we can't hide from God, but since He doesn't physically look us in the eye with the deep love and acceptance we need, He's chosen to do that through others.

Our challenge is simple: Since God knows your closets and you know yours as well, consider praying for—and pursuing—friendships with other men whom He can use to draw out the darkness and replace it with His light.

"The unexamined life never gets to the questions of what God wants us to do."

Man to Man

1. What are some of your concerns about sharing the contents of a dark closet with a group of Christian men?

2. What benefits would you expect to gain from joining and sharing in an accountability group?

3. Write down your fantasy about the operation of an ideal accountability group.

MEN AND THEIR FRIENDS

11

GIVING AWAY TIME YOU MAY NOT HAVE

Men and Serving

*O*kay, Yorkmeister, give us the next Top Ten list:

The Top Ten Reasons Why We Can Skip Church On Sunday

10 You gave last week.

9 Someone might call and invite you to go golfing.

8 It's impossible to record both the football game and "Meet the Press" at the same time.

7 Tomorrow's Monday.

6 The preachers on TV have better choirs, plus they don't mind if you snore during the sermons.

5 Since the Sabbath is supposed to be a day of rest, why not stay in bed?

A generous man will prosper; he who refreshes others will himself be refreshed.
Proverbs

4 The pastor might use you as a sermon illustration, and you don't want to mess up his talk by showing up.

3 Since the wife will be there and the Lord considers the two of you "one flesh," she's got you covered.

2 You need to keep an eye on those nosy neighbors across the street.

1 Chris Berman and ESPN SportsCenter.

Have you noticed that we roll out a Top Ten list right before we blast you with something really important? But the thing about church is that we're not supposed to show up Sunday morning and take up pew space like so many bumps on a log. Believe us, we *need* that hour or two each week.

God has big things in mind for us.

As members of the body of Christ, our goal is to flee our *selfish* nature and put on His *selfless* nature. The church plays a huge part in our ability to do this.

How do we start to learn unselfishness? By examining three things under our control:

1. Our time

2. Our possessions

3. The gifts God has entrusted us with

The men we interviewed were *huge* on giving time to the local church. Eighty-seven percent said they volunteer their hours, either as an elder, Bible study leader, Sunday school teacher, deacon, Awana teacher, usher, choir singer, or member of the finance committee. Some even did odd jobs around the church, such as plumbing, painting, and cleaning up!

For many, giving time to God was easier than spending time with Him. In our interviews, we asked men to tell us what they would give up *first* if life got

MEN AND SERVING

too hectic. (We'll tell you the first three responses in chapter 15, but no fair skipping ahead. You'll ruin the surprise.)

Fourth on the list was this: a set time of Scripture reading.

Fifth: a set time of prayer.

Sixth: looking for opportunities to share their faith.

Seventh: accountability (or close friendships) with other men.

Eighth: serving in the church.

Though disappointing, this was no stunning revelation. Numbers four through seven involve relationships with God and man. If you remember the last chapter, men aren't real motivated to do relational work; we'd rather keep people—and God—at arm's length.

This is especially true as those most important hours of the day slip from our grasp. We'll cut out God and forget about developing friendships before we'll drop our service to the church. Are we afraid of letting anyone, including God, get too close to us? Or are we driven more by fulfilling commitments (ones we shouldn't have made) than by bolstering our relationship with Christ and our fellow man?

For many of us, the answer to these questions is yes.

"As members of the body of Christ, our goal is to flee our selfish nature and put on His selfless nature."

Stepping Back

First of all, God's will is that you be holy and conform your life to the image of Jesus Christ. We can't do that without receiving what the church has to offer, and it can't be done without a genuine and growing relationship with God.

While His Word and the church help us recognize what we're supposed to *be*, some of us would rather skip that stage and just find out what we're supposed to *do*. Yes, it's true we can become more spiritual by doing unselfish things, but our nature would prefer it if we did Christian things that make us look like good Christians.

Some of the men we talked to were entrenched in heavy-duty Christian performance. One husband, with a ton of regrets, admitted that his tendency to work fifty to sixty hours a week *and* be a church volunteer took its toll.

"Because church was such a central part of our lives, my wife accepted my choices," he says. "We never had a blow-up, never saw a counselor, but I paid the price. Because I let my wife take the leadership, both at home and in our children's spiritual development, my kids and I can't relate to each other. They have become what their Dad was—very independent."

Another father told us, "The church has a way of making you feel guilty if you're not there every time the doors are open."

Making commitments to serve your church must be weighed carefully, especially when children are still at home. We've already made the point that once those precious hours escape, they're history. All too soon, those children we were entrusted with are walking out the door. Busy fathers *should* give their time to the church, but we must learn to serve strategically.

Thor was a perfect example of someone who failed to think through all the church asked him to do. After Thor became a Christian in his late twenties, he was eager to jump in with both feet. Within two years, he was spending Wednesday nights in youth ministry, teaching ninth-grade Sunday school, serving on the deacon board, participating in witnessing training, visiting newcomers on Sunday afternoons, *and* attending evangelism committee meetings. Whew! He took on all of this with a young daughter at home.

MEN AND SERVING

"I was at the point of burnout," he says. "During those years, my wife and I couldn't meet each other's needs. Things started to deteriorate romance-wise, too. My life was a mess.

"I'm the giver, but my wife's got the common sense of the family. Before things reached a peak, she insisted we talk and pray about it, to decide what areas we really wanted to serve in. The church never realized they were burning us out."

There's more insight into that last sentence than meets the eye. What Thor was saying is that most churches will never pick up that they're wearing out a willing member. In fact, they may not even want to know. When we asked twenty men with significant church involvement if they had ever been counseled to cut back or take time off, not one said yes.

We took this startling bit of information to a pastor for a reply. His answer cleared the air. "There's so much need," he began, "that a pastor often feels overwhelmed. He's desperate for help, and he knows believers give to feel productive. There's a delicate balance between getting things done and caring for the well-being of each person in your flock. It takes a mature pastor to deliberately hold a man back to make sure he's not overextended."

This pastor encourages church members to get involved in only one important ministry. "Even when I have a significant need, if a busy father volunteers, I tell him we're covered. While that policy has left glaring holes at times, I'm determined not to allow that guy to burn out. My policy works . . . most of the time."

"Making commitments to serve your church must be weighed carefully, especially when children are still at home."

Recognizing Pressures

A father who thinks through his church commitments will reap the benefits for decades. And pastors who understand the condition of their overtaxed fathers will also benefit.

We know ministers with this healthy attitude, but most of them head large churches, where the volunteer pool is larger. Pastors of small churches don't always have that luxury.

If you're smart, you'll recognize that the subtle pressures from pastors or elder board members doesn't mean you have to say yes. And when it comes to making the most of those hours away from work, you really need to follow His direction!

We recommend that you sit down with your pastor and discuss two things:

1. *How many hours a month can I afford to give?* Of course, certain times of the year are better than others, but there will be times when you'll have to cut back your volunteer hours.

2. *What are my spiritual gifts?* If your pastor knows them (those God-given attributes discussed in Romans 12, Ephesians 4, and 1 Corinthians 12), then he can help you find out what's the best ministry for you. If he's not aware of your spiritual gifts, then discuss areas where you might be most effective. Sometimes the pastor may give you a test that can evaluate what your spiritual gifts might be.

Once you've got a handle on your time, a few things will happen:

- *You'll find it easier to say "no thank you," to long-term commitments that don't fit your gifts or your heart for ministry.* One man, Harv, is certainly busy enough—he's the father of six children. But he's felt called to minister to others and introduce them to the basics of the Christian life. He's chosen two areas to put his time into:

MEN AND SERVING

teaching Sunday school and working with a jail ministry every other week. If he's called to serve on a building fund committee, Harv can, without feeling guilty, say he's already committed.

- *You'll still be in a position to say yes to short-term church projects.* Jerry loves to serve in his small church. He knows a lot has to be done, but there aren't many warm bodies to tackle projects. While he's careful about agreeing to serve on "nonproductive, long-term committees," Jerry gladly sets up chairs or makes last-minute phone calls. Because he's not overcommitted, he can respond at a moment's notice—and he's glad to!

- *You'll actually enjoy giving your time.* In fact, you'll even look forward to it! Bruce was one father who couldn't say no. It wasn't long before he was doing more and enjoying it less. After trying to fulfill everyone else's agenda, Bruce found out he liked leading a "Discovery"-type group for non-Christian men. Gradually, he left the other committees to spend time preparing his class lessons. Not only that, he was an excellent teacher. Bruce is now the guy his church goes to when they know a non-Christian who needs help.

- *Your ministry, no matter how small you think it is, will have God's blessing because you're operating in your gifted areas.* A busy Southern California entrepreneur, who works a lot of hours, has a heart that beats for the inner city. But he doesn't have time to drive downtown and still keep up his family life. So he spends what little free time he has on the phone learning more about worthy ministries. He supports them financially, and his business contacts have allowed him to do some fund raising, as well. In just a few hours each week, this man is making an incredible impact.

Getting Creative

Phil also wanted to teach junior high guys, so he took on a Sunday school class for eighth-graders. About six months into his commitment, the pastor called and told him the church had an opening on the elder board. "You're the logical choice," said the pastor.

While Phil didn't mind the extra Sunday morning duty, he couldn't hack another night away from his family. He said he'd join the board if they held their meetings every other week before his Wednesday night youth group. They agreed.

Phil's quick thinking meant he could be part of three separate ministries at the "cost" of only one night a week. Time management never felt so good!

Andrew, a family physician, teaches a Sunday school class for high school boys ("The only time they're interested in what I have to say is when we talk about sex," he laughs), but he found a week-in and week-out commitment too daunting. So Andrew team-teaches the class with another colleague. That way, when he's out of town or on vacation, he's covered.

Rick wanted to spend more time with his kids when they hit those all-important teen years, but he didn't know diddly about relating to them. His spiritual gift was being an encourager, so Rick started a support group for the youth pastor. Each month, a group of parents gathered to pray for the kids and the youth leadership team. They also volunteered their time for the big youth events.

After a couple years, Rick had developed a love for teens he'd never had before. While supporting the youth team, he also picked up a few ideas on how to talk with them. When his children reached junior high, Rick fit right in with the youth group—and didn't come off as a geek. Rick found the right combi-

MEN AND SERVING

nation of church service and spending time with his teenagers.

For Those Too Busy to Give Anything

The key to an abundant Christian life is giving. While many men would rather give money than time—and some can do only that—knowing the joy of directly meeting someone else's needs is beyond compare. We must be men in constant search for the elusive key to servant-style Christianity: balance.

So far, we've only talked about the hazards of overcommitment to the church. But there are thousands of men who should be giving their time and abilities to the Lord—but flat-out aren't. They've mastered the art of saying no to pleas for help ("Gee, Bill, I'm busy all this week"). These are the men who have slid by, nearly invisible to the rest of the congregation.

Why don't these men give of themselves?

They haven't matured to the productive stage. Children need time to grow before they can do even the simplest of tasks. It's the same with Christians. Unfortunately, some men who've attended church for years still haven't caught on to the abundant life they will receive when they give sacrificially. Often, recreation is their priority, not meeting the needs of others.

If you're stingy with volunteering your time, be encouraged. It's not too late. The first step is to meet with a trusted member of your church, someone you admire, and tell him you'd like to get your feet wet. Get involved with something you'd enjoy doing, but start small (try to skip time-consuming committee work). Once you're caught up in a ministry, you'll wonder why you waited so long. Meeting the needs of others is infectious. Then you'll have to reread the

"We must be men in constant search for the elusive key to servant-style Christianity: balance."

beginning of this chapter to discover how not to get overcommitted!

Man to Man

1. Can you figure out how many hours a week you give to the church? How many of those hours are fixed? How many are flexible?

2. If you believe you are overcommitted to church activities, where can you begin to cut back? You might develop a plan for using the time you want to give to the church more constructively.

3. If you believe you are undercommitted to church work, identify programs you would like to work with and prioritize those programs. Or outline a program or ministry that you might initiate for your church.

MEN AND SERVING

12

REACH OUT AND TOUCH SOMEBODY

Men and Influencing Their World

*L*et's start with a couple of Top Five lists this
time, since sharing our faith isn't exactly grist for
"Late Night with David Letterman."

The Top Five Kinds
Of Neighbors You Should
Avoid Sharing Your Faith With

5 First-week insurance sales reps working for
a company you've never heard of.

4 Islamic fundamentalists who are visiting
from Baghdad.

3 The crotchety old guy next door who hates
your dog—and your kids.

2 Pit bull owners.

1 AWA's (Atheists with Attitudes).

*"Come, follow
me," Jesus said,
"and I will make
you fishers of
men."*
Matthew

*The fruit of the
righteous is a tree
of life, and he who
wins souls is wise.*
Proverbs

The Top Five
Co-Workers You Should
Avoid Sharing Your Faith With

5 Anybody who's seen you sneak into work late, leave early, or waste company time around the water cooler.

4 Anyone who perks up when office conversations turn to the latest TV evangelist scandal.

3 The guy they promoted you over.

2 The "brother" who adopted Islamic first and last names.

1 The boss ("You think I need Jesus? I think you need a new job!").

Before coming to Focus on the Family as editor of the *Breakaway* teen magazine, I (Greg) spent ten years as a "professional Christian." That is, I raised financial support so I could be a full-time missionary to teenagers through Youth for Christ.

Sharing my faith with teens and their families was my life. I loved it. I was always trying to create opportunities to build new relationships or explain my faith to those ready to hear. I welcomed the challenge of making a friendship, winning the right to be heard, sharing the gospel, and then seeing new Christians become integrated into a church.

Winning souls was the ultimate—until I changed careers.

My decision to leave Youth for Christ wasn't easy, but I couldn't raise enough support to keep my wife home with the kids. When the call came from Focus on the Family, it looked like the right move.

Moving from clean, pristine Seattle to smoggy Los Angeles was just as much a shock as the shift from missionary to magazine editor. Nor was I used to working a straight eight to five and commuting ninety minutes a day. Learning a new job and spending too many hours on the L.A. freeways sapped my desire to think about anything beyond my own family. Slowly, my motivation to read the Bible and pray decreased. I became "satisfied" with spending a few minutes each week with God.

One Saturday, while rummaging through the garage, I discovered some devotional notebooks I'd written during my quiet times from years past. I flipped one open and began reading. An hour later I was still turning pages. I suddenly realized my relationship with God was distant. And He wasn't the one who'd moved.

That afternoon in the garage helped me understand where I was with God—and where I used to be. I no longer hungered to spend time with the Lord. The reason? I didn't need the same amount of spiritual food because I wasn't exercising my spiritual gifts. I had reached a point of constipation. I'm sure God was a little nauseated at my behavior too!

Keeping Fit

When I worked for Youth for Christ, I exercised my faith each day and tried to stay in top spiritual shape. My sharing skills were put to the test every day. But when I left Y.F.C., my faith atrophied from insufficient use. Once I realized what was going on, I had a choice. I could:

1. *Maintain the status quo*—The easy route was to convince myself that my days of converting teens were in the past. Heck, my kids were getting older, and something always needed to be done around the house. Besides, I knew

"I didn't need the same amount of spiritual food because I wasn't exercising my spiritual gifts."

from my decade in Y.F.C. that it usually took months to yield any results. The same went for friends outside the church, but there it could take *years* before you'd see them turn to Christ.

2. *Or, I could make myself uncomfortable*—Fortunately, I'd been in Southern California only a few months when I found those journals in the garage. I decided I needed to be around a few men who swear once in a while.

After telling God I meant business, I asked Him to put me back into the game. Within weeks, two things happened:

First, I started coaching my son's T-ball team. Out of thirteen kids, ours was the only family who went to church. Perfect.

My goals were simple: to teach the kids how to hold a bat, field a grounder, run the bases—and to build a bridge to one or two other men. My wife, Elaine, completed the "double play" by becoming team mom.

It wasn't long before we clicked with another family, but it wasn't our goal to make them a "project." They would see right through that. Though they really needed what Christ could offer them, we simply wanted to be their friends.

Over sixteen months, this family, with a background in a "guilt-producing traditional church," saw that our faith was far different than anything they'd been exposed to.

Elaine quietly invited the wife to join her weekly Bible study—and she accepted! We continued to reach out, and when we moved to Colorado Springs in the summer of 1991, we waved goodbye to friends who were open to the gospel, though they've yet to make the complete leap of faith.

MEN AND INFLUENCING THEIR WORLD

Second, I decided I'd make an effort to befriend a neighbor or two. Unfortunately, our neighborhood was equipped with friend-proof contraptions called garage-door openers. Before I could barely wave hello, men could drive into their homes—all except Joe across the street. His garage was like mine, too junky to hold both cars, so he had to park outside. All we had in common was we were married and each had two kids.

For the first couple of months we made small talk. Then Christmas season arrived, and instead of inviting Joe and his family to church, we asked them to join us on a nighttime trip to see the Christmas lights in a nearby suburb. They agreed to go, and that evening we gawked at thousands of lights strung up by families in this particular neighborhood. Many of the front yards were decked out with elaborate displays. Some told the story of Christ's birth. That one night proved to be the start of a great friendship.

I soon found out that Joe had absolutely no spiritual background and that his wife, Cheryl, had gone to church as a child. By answering questions and making them a part of our lives, we were there when Joe and Cheryl committed their lives to Christ.

What these stories illustrate was a simple decision to be *available*. The outcome, of course, was up to God. But the results He accomplished might not have occurred if I hadn't felt spiritually constipated and decided the best medicine was to do something about it. Once my spiritual pulse quickened, I began spending more time with God.

Overcoming Obstacles

As the years roll by and life remains hectic, I sometimes lose my desire to reach out to others. My pursuit

MEN AND INFLUENCING THEIR WORLD

of security and "making a life" for our family causes me to think inward, not outward. Once I'm in the groove, it's tough to break habits.

Some of the fathers we interviewed agreed. "Trying to communicate your faith is work," said a Texas father. "I'm naturally shy, so I have a hard time expressing something that's close to me. I try to get involved in people's lives at work, but I've never personally led someone to the Lord. Mostly, I've planted seeds. When I *have* prayed for courage to talk to them about Christ point-blank, it didn't work too well. I didn't get a strong rejection, but when we got to a certain point in the conversation they'd say, 'I know where this is leading to. I'm just not interested.' "

Important Fact #1

No matter how many "won-to-the-Lord" stories you've heard, most Christians will never lead someone to Christ in their lifetimes. This isn't meant to get you off the hook, but to take some of the guilt off. When I brought this issue up with a Georgia lumberman one afternoon, he said, "I'm not responsible for the results. We're not called to convert people, but to share with them when the situation arises. It's up to God to bring them home."

Your job is to say, "Today, Lord, I want you to use me to bring someone one step closer to You."

Important Fact #2

Many executives work from a company mission statement. They know it keeps their work priorities on target as they set the day's agenda. The same holds true for Christian fathers.

When we asked the fathers what they felt was the mission of a Christian, their responses fit into two categories:

142

1. *Being*—A Christian should act like who he is: loving, kind, compassionate, holy, faithful, and wise.

2. *Doing*—A Christian knows we weren't put here on earth just to pass through life. Rather, we are to be wise stewards of our talents and gifts, fulfilling the Great Commission to tell the whole world about God's gift of Jesus Christ.

Important Fact #3

God has given every Christian a network. While we all have friends and acquaintances who are believers, many of us socialize and work with plenty of non-churched people.

As we mentioned in chapter 10, busy men have a tendency to keep relationships on a professional level. For most of us, our childhood training or our father's modeling taught us to keep other men at arm's length. Indeed, our culture expects men not to get too friendly. We're socialized into believing we're at a disadvantage if we reveal what's behind the mask.

Dropping Your Guard

Until we start dropping the macho act, our network isn't going to see Christ working in our lives. Go ahead, drop your guard. Being genuine can be fun.

Sam, a Detroit executive, wanted a co-worker to see Jesus Christ for who He really is. One day over lunch, Sam began talking about things he had never shared with this co-worker: his discomfort with being overweight; the troubles his oldest son was having in school; and his strained relationship with his brother.

"Go ahead, drop your guard. Being genuine can be fun."

MEN AND INFLUENCING THEIR WORLD

What Can I Ask My Neighbors If I Want To Gauge Their Spiritual Temperature?

1. Does your family have any special Christmas traditions?
2. What do you like to do on the weekends?
3. Has your family ever gone to church?
4. Are your kids going to Sunday school?
5. Would you and your family be interested in seeing our great Christmas (or Easter) program at church?

After You Find Out Their Interest Level In Spiritual Matters, More Personal Questions Can Be Asked, Such As:

1. Have you ever read parts of the Bible in a modern translation?
2. What do you think God is like?
3. Do you think Jesus really existed? May I tell you who the Bible says He is?
4. What do you think a Christian is? May I explain the difference between a Christian and someone who's religious?
5. Have you had any bad experiences with Christians or with a church? Have your parents had any bad experiences? Have you had any good experiences?

By communicating seemingly small stuff in an upbeat way, Sam demonstrated a level of honesty uncharacteristic of other men around the office. It wasn't long before the other guy began to share *his* struggles with Sam.

Sam's conscious choice to take the first step of openness resulted not only in the man's becoming a Christian, but two other fellows as well. Now they meet weekly to help each other grow in the faith.

Our network of co-workers and neighbors is the mission field God has given us outside of our home. Believe it or not, it's even more important than our company's mission.

How to Make It Happen

Here are a few practical ideas men shared with us.

Serving

Serve co-workers and neighbors. "Though I'm not a mechanic, I help people with their car problems," said Lester. "It's never a burden for me because it's an area of ministry that fits like a glove."

Have people lined up at Lester's door to pray to receive Christ after he's installed new brake pads on the Toyota? No, but that's not his goal. By working on people's cars, Lester's building relationships and demonstrating servanthood. One day, he'll be able to turn the corner and discuss things more eternal than oil changes.

Planting

Plant the seeds of truth. Tell your friends about discovery-type classes your church may offer. The teachers can answer tough questions about faith and what it means to be a Christian. Another way to interest nonbelievers is to ask them to join you for church concerts, weeknight services, church sports leagues, and children's events.

MEN AND INFLUENCING THEIR WORLD

"Our network of co-workers and neighbors is the mission field God has given us outside of our home."

Inviting

Invite another couple with common interests (sports, hobbies, or kids the same age) over for dinner. Usually an evening of social talk will allow you to take their spiritual temperature. When the goal isn't sharing the plan of salvation, the pressure's off.

One father said he often sought out the spiritual condition of his neighbors. He did small things to build friendships, then he stayed in touch well enough to know if emergency needs came up. Once a neighbor's mother passed away, and he and his family were the first to offer to watch the kids and bring over a few meals. That made a statement to the neighbor about a deeper level of concern.

Sam never misses a trick with his Illinois neighbors. For Halloween, he hands out tracts with the candy. Each tract begins, "Dear Trick-or-Treater . . ." and then gently shares God's message of love. "The idea has gone around," says Sam. "In fact, I saw our tract being used by a different church. We try to be like the Apostle Paul, who adapted the message to his audience."

Sam is even more—how should we say this?— original each Easter. On the Saturday before the Resurrection, Sam dresses up in an Easter bunny suit. Then he hops his six-foot, two-inch frame from house to house, depositing homemade sweet rolls at each home. "I tell everyone that I'm delivering the sweet rolls that night so I won't disturb them during church services the following morning." Ah, Sam, you're so subtle. Who wouldn't remember to attend Easter services with that reminder?

Another family asked the neighborhood parents if they could borrow their kids to make a video of the Christmas story. Nearly all agreed and, of course, the kids loved the idea. The parents gathered a few props and shot the video in about three hours one Saturday afternoon. When it was time to screen the Big Event, all the parents showed up as though it were a Hollywood premiere. What parent wouldn't want to see their child on the silver—make that TV—screen?

Without handing out a tract or inviting neighbors to a church service, this family made their faith known. Afterward, some of the neighbors even thought that attending a Christmas Eve service might be a good idea. *Hmmm.*

The day before Easter, two families that lived close together sent flyers around the neighborhood announcing a Saturday morning Easter egg hunt. After the kids had scrounged through bushes for the elusive eggs, the parents handed out refreshments and led the kids in Christian songs. Several parents hung around, including a few dads, and they heard a brief message on the real meaning of Easter to top off the egg hunt.

The most powerful way to communicate your faith is to tell your own story. Explaining what Christ means to you in your own words rarely sounds phony or rehearsed.

Many unchurched couples have dozens of misconceptions about God and the Bible. While you may be asked to walk them through the basics, they won't be convinced by dogma. It's more likely that they'll be interested in hearing how God has made a difference in your life.

Many of you may feel more comfortable sharing your faith with co-workers than with family. In fact, our survey showed that 91 percent felt the same way. Sharing with relatives was second at 80 percent, which is still very high. About half the fathers (48 percent) said they talk to their neighbors about their faith, and 40 percent talk to strangers.

MEN AND INFLUENCING THEIR WORLD

"The most powerful way to communicate your faith is to tell your own story."

147

Some Questions to Ask

Look around your church service next Sunday and notice the teenagers slumped in the pews. Then look at your own children and ask yourself:

- Do I want my kids to have a faith that's in their heads, but not in their hearts?
- Do I want my children to relate to those outside the church?
- Would I be satisfied if all they had were Christian friends?
- Do I want them to have a deep concern for those who are living only for this world?
- Do I want them to care deeply about the eternity of others?

During our "season" of childrearing, we'll either demonstrate an indifference to those who don't know Christ, or we'll show a genuine desire to care and to share His love.

And that's all God's calling us to do.

Man to Man

1. What have you done about sharing your faith up to this point?

2. Which ideas for sharing your faith do you feel will be useful for you? Do you have other ideas?

3. Have you felt that God requires you to bring your contacts through to a profession of faith? How might knowing that God does not call you to convert someone, but rather to share your faith with them, change your relationship to pre-Christians?

MEN AND INFLUENCING THEIR WORLD

148

13

BROTHER, CAN YOU SPARE SOME TIME FOR GOD?

Men and Their God, Part II

*H*i, Greg, this is your conscience speaking.

Who me? What do you want this time?

I just thought I'd bug you, Greg. You know, you haven't read your Bible this week.

But I've been *beaucoup* busy. The boys had a soccer tournament last weekend, and I had to mow the lawn after work. Last night Elaine and I went out for a pizza. We haven't done something like that in a month. . . .

If finding time to spend with your family wasn't guilt-loading enough, try adding *spending time with God* to the equation. This is tricky territory, but we didn't want to close our book without making you feel guilty at least one more time. (Just kidding.)

If our little opener didn't grab you, then here are a few more questions to clobber the ol' conscience:

- If God's the most important person in your life, why don't you spend more time with Him?

So then, just as you received Christ Jesus as Lord, continue to live in him, rooted and built up in him, strengthened in the faith as you were taught, and overflowing with thankfulness.

Colossians

- How will your kids ever grasp the importance of reading God's Word if they never see you crack open a Bible?
- Can you be the spiritual leader if you don't have family devotions?
- With the way our culture celebrates those who spurn God, aren't you motivated to cancel your cable TV and to start spending an hour a day with God?

No?
I wonder why?

"If finding time to spend with your family wasn't guilt-loading enough, try adding spending time with God to the equation."

MEN AND THEIR GOD, PART II

What God Really Wants

Salvation is a big deal to God. After Adam and Eve made the wrong choices in the Garden of Eden, God was gracious enough to send the Redeemer our way. He willingly allowed His only Son to suffer and die a criminal's death on a cross that should have been reserved for us.

If you believe Christ's death was God's way of paying for our disobedience, you might ask, "What else does He want?"

This simple question can be answered in a dozen ways. Though it's outside the scope of this book to tell you everything God wants, you can count on one thing: *He wants one step more than we're giving Him now.*

The Apostle Paul usually complimented the recipients of his letters, but then always issued challenges such as this one: "Finally, brothers, we instructed you how to live in order to please God, as in fact you are living. Now we ask you and urge you in the Lord Jesus to do this more and more" (1 Thessalonians 4:1). Another version says to "excel still more."

Instead of wagging a finger or assuming you've lost your motivation to seek God, let's do a little heart check on several major issues.

Someone's Waiting for You

Who do you think wants to spend time with you every day?

- The God who didn't answer that one desperate childhood prayer when you really needed Him?
- The God who's only interested in handing down a bunch of killjoy rules?
- The God who expects you to attend an hour of boring ritual so He'll like you better?
- The God who doesn't love you anymore because you've done some raunchy stuff in the past?
- The God who carefully made you, is constantly with you, was willing to die for you, and literally can't wait to have a small chunk of your time to remind you how important you are to Him?

Get the picture?

If you're not motivated to spend time with God, then perhaps you've got the wrong idea about the God you're spending time with. Take, for example, those with no knowledge of the Lord. If they really knew how God felt about them, they wouldn't stay outside the church for long, right? But the same misconceptions that hold them back often keep us from Him as well.

Imagine what it would be like if your children avoided you because they weren't sure what you were like. Naturally, you'd be hurt, but you'd definitely try to do what you could to clear up the problem.

"If you're not motivated to spend time with God, then perhaps you've got the wrong idea about the God you're spending time with."

MEN AND THEIR GOD, PART II

151

MEN AND THEIR GOD, PART II

Wake-Up Call

Roger spent eight months designing a complicated new test instrument for an Oregon electronics company. During this long stretch, he never got more than five hours of sleep each night. His work life in chaos, Roger barely had time for himself, but he managed to keep his eyes on God.

"When the project came to an end," he says, "management hadn't done their job securing future contracts, so most of them ended up resigning. Over the next two years, people were fired every week. I never knew if I'd have a job by the end of the day. I went into periods of depression that had some fairly bad effects on my wife. Needless to say, there was a lot of tension.

"Those two years were tough, but I grew spiritually more than I ever had before. The Psalms became alive because the writer went through the same emotions I was going through. I knew God understood and cared about the situation I was in."

Did Roger's dependence on God mean he wanted to spend more time with Him later on when times got better? It should have, but it didn't. "I just kinda got back into my old rut of being real inconsistent. I could blame a lot of things, but I guess I didn't want it bad enough."

Why do we do that to Him? Either we're:

1. stupid
2. lulled to sleep by Satan
3. think God is most helpful when times are tough
4. all of the above

You guessed it. It's number 4, all of the above.

Code of Conduct

If you became a Christian semi-recently, you might recall how easy it was to start reading the Word. Everything about God was fresh, and you hungered to learn everything you could about Him. In addition, you genuinely wanted to please God and do what was right. It never seemed like a chore to pore through your Bible.

At the same time, you learned how to pray and humble yourself to the Lord. You slowly realized that

---

Top Ten Worst Reasons For Not Reading the Bible

10 There aren't enough action photos.

9 Once you've read the blood-and-guts box scores in the Old Testament, loaves and fishes aren't too exciting.

8 Anything they can make a kids' version out of can't be too important.

7 If I start studying the Bible, it won't be long before I'm not learning from my pastor's sermons anymore.

6 The New Testament is all Greek—even to the best of seminary students.

5 I can wait for the movie version.

4 If I act as though I know what I'm talking about, someone might ask me to lead a Sunday school class.

3 The book has been seen in a lot of seedy motel rooms.

2 It was written in code—if you don't have the ring, you can't understand it.

1 It was written by a bunch of foreigners.

MEN AND THEIR GOD, PART II

God not only listened, but He actually answered your requests.

As our hairlines travel north and our bellies slope south, so does our walk with God recede into flabbiness. Some of us don't feel the need to tackle timeless truths. After years of sermons, Sunday school classes, and Bible studies, we've already "learned" everything God has to tell us, so our Christian life becomes, well . . . boring.

Reading the Bible is tiresome if it's our habit to treat it simply as a rulebook for behavior. Though learning precepts and principles is essential to becoming more mature in Christ, it's dangerous to go through life thinking that God's Word is only there to instruct us.

Think about it: How would you feel if one of your children came to you *only* when he or she wanted to know right from wrong? You'd be crushed. You'd feel undervalued, and parenting wouldn't be any fun!

Above all, God wants to have a good time with us. Though He's not a jokester (it *is* tough to kid around with someone we can't see), He longs for us to invite Him into every situation we face. That's what praying "without ceasing" is all about (1 Thessalonians 5:17, NKJV).

> **"As our hairlines travel north and our bellies slope south, so does our walk with God recede into flabbiness."**

MEN AND THEIR GOD, PART II

Doing That Devotional Thing

In our survey we asked our fathers how often they read their Bibles. The results:

- not at all—2 percent
- once a month—6 percent
- once a week—8 percent
- several times a week—47 percent
- daily—37 percent

In other words, 84 percent of the surveyed fathers said they read their Bibles regularly. More interesting, however, were the responses to our follow-up question: "Are you satisfied with this amount?" Only 23 percent said yes, while 22 percent answered "sometimes." The rest (55 percent) said no.

Many of our fathers expressed frustration with the amount of time they were able to read their Bibles and with the discipline it entailed. Here's how one father described it: "I don't find Bible reading to be a relaxing, recreational pastime. I need to be studying, but I feel I'm under pressure to read."

Jerry shared his shortcomings: "The Word preaches that you have to be consistent. That's where I fall short."

Not too many years ago I (Greg) thought if I read my Bible every single day, my relationship with God would be great. I bought a leather-bound journal and recorded everything I read. I went twenty months straight—that's over six hundred days—without missing a day in God's Word. Finally, I intentionally broke the streak. I no longer wanted to be the Cal Ripken of Bible reading. (Besides, I had no Lou Gehrig to shoot for.)

Why did I stop reading? Because "the streak" became more important than my relationship with the Lord. We shouldn't read the Bible because it's the spiritual thing to do, nor should we legalistically follow every hidden biblical principle just because some conference speaker or Sunday school teacher said it's the only way to be a true Christian. Doing so reduces our relationship with God to our own effort. It robs us of the joy of being rightly related to Him.

Throughout my years in the ministry, I've seen many people go through similar stages of

- initial acceptance and excitement
- hunger for God and His Word

- desire to share their faith
- passing and failing tests God allows to come their way to strengthen their faith
- identifying with God and the Body of Christ for a lifetime
- growing through normal ups and downs

These following two stages usually arrive within five years. Both are normal, but each is an immature step toward maintaining and sharing our relationship with God:

1. We become bored with the routine, but entrenched both in Christian attitudes and in social relationships to the point where we are "satisfied" with the status quo; and

2. Although we're more committed, we also become more legalistic as we begin to measure our own spirituality—and the spirituality of others—based on our actions as Christians.

A Deeper Level

The final stage, the place where God longs for us to be, is friendship. At this point, we finally reach the level of enjoying God. As we pursue Him, He shares the depths of who He is. It's a process that doesn't stop until the day we meet Him face to face.

On the eve of Christ's crucifixion and after He had spent nearly three years with the disciples, Jesus said these words: "I no longer call you servants, because a servant does not know his master's business. Instead, I have called you friends, for everything that I learned from my Father I have made known to you" (John 15:15).

How does this relate to your kids? If you're a diligent parent, you spend years teaching correct behavior: how to treat others, having good table manners, keeping clean and groomed. These disciplines help keep them on track. But often, when the kids reach their early teens (around ages fourteen to sixteen), the parent begins moving from teacher to counselor. This transfer of responsibility—from your shoulders to your child's—continues until they reach adulthood.

Eventually, what every loving mother and father hopes for is to be one of the child's best friends. Did you notice that this progression is nearly identical to the one Jesus described in the passage above?

An Ohio pastor remembers hearing a talk by Chuck Swindoll, also a pastor and host of the radio program "Insight for Living."

"Chuck once said, 'It took four years to get through seminary—and fourteen years to get over it,' " recalls the minister. "I spent eight years in school using the Bible as a textbook. There was no joy of discovery anymore. Today my goal isn't to read a certain amount of chapters. My goal is to meet with the Lord on a daily basis. Psalm 42:1 says, 'As the deer pants for streams of water, so my soul pants for you, O God.'

"The question I had to ask was: *Do I want a relationship with the Lord, or do I just want to spend time with a book?* That realization has taken me to another level of understanding His character. The Word has become more vital and alive than it's ever been."

A federal government employee from Washington, D.C., says he tries not to separate his spiritual life from his day-to-day routines—eating, going to work, talking with his wife, and playing with his kids. "It's all an act of stewardship and worship. Sometimes when we go to the beach, we read the Bible. Whenever God is in the center, it's a spiritual activity."

Admittedly, being God's friend can be a tough concept to grasp, especially for those who believe a daily quiet time is the ultimate measure for how

"Do I want a relationship with the Lord, or do I just want to spend time with a book?"

you're doing spiritually. If we don't, then one of two things will occur:

1. We'll convince ourselves we're more spiritual than others because we're reading or praying a certain amount of time each day.
2. We'll feel guilty because compared to others or what we used to do, we're not measuring up.

It becomes a relationship by performance. Not only was I once caught in this low level of spiritual maturity, I used to teach it!

While a daily quiet time with the Lord is one way to measure how you're doing spiritually, we need to go beyond just regularly reading the Bible. Let me tell a little story.

I grew up spending family vacations along the Oregon coast. We usually stayed in a little beach cottage in the town of Neskowin. One of my favorite pastimes was to go beachcombing. The biggest treasure of all was finding a perfect sand dollar, one with no chips or cracks. They were always difficult to find.

A couple of summers ago, I took my family back to Neskowin, and my sister, Gail, and her son, Aaron, joined us. The sand dollar hunt was on. Our first morning, we slept in and headed down the beach around 9:00 A.M., looking for sand dollars that had washed up on shore. Though we searched hard for perfect sand dollars, we were skunked. The next day the same thing happened—*nada*. We were getting discouraged.

On the third day, I saw a lady with a bag full of shells walking up the beach. Many of them looked like whole sand dollars.

"Where'd you find all those shells?"

"Down the beach a mile or two," she replied.

Aha! I wasn't going far enough! Then a thought hit me: *Even if I walk all the way down there, that lady,*

MEN AND THEIR GOD, PART II

or someone else, has already beaten me to the good shells. But if I get up earlier than everyone tomorrow . . . I'll find the treasure before they do.

The next morning, we arose at the crack of dawn—5:30 A.M. We were determined to find perfect sand dollars. With the tide ebbing, we had plenty of new territory to scour. But after walking three-quarters of a mile down the beach, we'd found only one or two. My sister tired and returned to the beach rental. Aaron and I decided to press on.

About one hundred yards farther, we hit the mother lode. Within a thirty-foot radius we found a dozen whole perfect sand dollars. We were in hog heaven! Were there any more?

We continued to walk, keeping our eyes fixed on the sand. More sand dollars popped up! We collected more than 125 perfect sand dollars. But the effort pooped us out; it was a two-mile walk to the sand dollar cache, which meant a four-mile round trip in the soft sand.

Yet we were rewarded. Spurred by our success, we repeated the hunt the next morning and found 150 more! After that, we felt we'd better give the other tourists a chance to find a few.

About a week later, I was spending quiet time with the Lord when the lesson hit me:

1. We wanted treasure.

2. We got up earlier.

3. We traveled farther.

4. We exceeded our goals beyond our wildest dreams.

The parable works like this: First, treasure with God is an attitude. Do I value God enough to do whatever it takes to meet with Him? That's not a time question, but rather a heart question.

Second, finding treasure with God takes discipline. Locating a quiet spot to reflect on Him is no easy task. It may mean getting up earlier in the morning.

Third, God's treasure is not found by scanning a quick chapter or whispering a one-minute prayer. It's found, as James says, when we "come near to God." The result? "He will come near to you."

In my own personal time with God, I treasure Him *most* after my heart has been genuinely drawn near to Him. Sometimes it happens as soon as I open His Word. More often it occurs when I go farther . . . and let Him know I desire to find His treasure.

Last, when we walk the extra mile, God will show us how much of a treasure He is.

If we don't move beyond our notion that time with God means fifteen minutes in a devotional book and a structured prayer list, we'll always feel we don't have a friendship with God. Maximizing our day means inviting our best Friend into every hour, every situation, every worry, and all the "spare" time we have. That way, we can walk a little farther down the beach and discover the treasure He has waiting for us.

Man to Man

1. Recall the excitement with which you read God's Word in the months after your conversion. Be specific about your times for reading Scripture then.

2. Think about how you can make Scripture reading exciting today. What life issues can the Bible bring light to for you?

3. What benefits can you hope to gain from walking "the extra mile" in searching God's Word?

"Do I value God enough to do whatever it takes to meet with Him? That's not a time question, but rather a heart question."

MEN AND THEIR GOD, PART II

160

14

EVERY HOME IS A STAGE

Men and Their Modeling

When I (Mike) lived in Southern California, our family developed an odd Christmas tradition. No, we didn't go to the beach and bury a pig in the sand for a Yuletide luau, but we started doing something nearly as strange.

Each December 24, Nicole and I took the kids to Disneyland, a thirty-minute drive from our home. Before you gasp—as my Swiss in-laws did—let me explain. The day before Christmas draws a relatively light crowd to the Magic Kingdom. Christmas Eve is also one of the few days each winter that Disneyland opens at 8:00 A.M. (The rest of the time the amusement park has a 10:00 A.M. start.)

Many tourists are not aware of the early opening. We learned to arrive just before eight o'clock, and for two, three hours, we had the park to ourselves. Andrea and Patrick never had it so good.

Disneyland started to pack out about noon, just in time for a lunch break. We usually hung around until the afternoon Christmas parade, and then we made a beeline home.

Fathers, do not exasperate your children; instead, bring them up in the training and instruction of the Lord.

Ephesians

Our tradition didn't end there. We dressed up for the 6:00 P.M. candlelight Christmas Eve church service. Then we returned home for a special Swiss dinner of *raclette*, melted cheese over boiled potatoes.

I will never forget December 24, 1990. We did our usual Disneyland routine, then rushed home in time for the candlelight Christmas Eve service. Early in the program, assistant pastor Tarryl Bockelman asked all the children to walk to the front and sit around him for the children's sermon. Andrea, then seven, and Patrick, then six, bounded to the front.

Tarryl took a few wrapped presents out of a shopping bag. The children's eyes doubled in size—they probably thought they were going to get an early gift! When Tarryl asked if they were going to open Christmas presents in the morning, they all yelled, "Yes!"

Then he asked the children if they had bought presents for their parents. The "yeses" weren't so loud.

"You know, there is one present you can give your parents that would be the best present in the whole wide world. You can ask Jesus into your heart and become a Christian tonight. Believe me, that's the best present you could ever give your mom and dad."

Tarryl's little sermon touched me—and got me to thinking. *Is it time to ask my kids if they want to make a commitment to Christ?*

That evening, as we ate our *raclette*, I asked Andrea and Patrick what they thought about Tarryl's talk.

"You know, if you ask Jesus into your heart, He assures you that you will go to heaven," I prompted, wondering where the conversation would go.

"We know, Daddy," said Andrea.

"Do you know how to become a Christian?"

"Yes, we do," replied Andrea, again speaking for her brother.

"Well, would you like to ask Jesus into your heart?"

MEN AND THEIR MODELING

162

Andrea nodded yes, as did Patrick. The kids turned rather solemn, as befitted the occasion.

I took a deep breath and silently asked God for the right words. Asking them to repeat after me, I led my two children to the Lord. Inside, I told myself that I was a fortunate father to witness such a wonderful thing.

And now the Yorkey family has a new tradition: celebrating the kids' spiritual "birthday" every Christmas Eve.

Passing the Baton

No one says it better than Dr. Dobson when it comes to the importance of fathers and mothers "passing the baton" of faith to their children. Teaching our children a saving knowledge of Jesus Christ is *the* most important task we fathers have set before us.

The dads we interviewed agreed. "If, at the end of my life, I haven't transmitted my belief in Christ to my children, then I haven't been faithful to the calling God has given to me," said Ronnie, the California CPA. "The bottom line isn't this world, but will my son be on the other side?"

Chuck said his most satisfying moment came when his two young daughters, Ann and Wendy, accepted Christ as their Lord. "You can do everything you can to lead them to that decision, but you can't force them to do it," he said.

Roy modeled Christian behavior to set the stage for his children. "I tried to raise my children in a Christian home by always saying a blessing before meals and talking to them about how Jesus is always with them."

Some children have their own spiritual awakening timetable, and all a father can do is be there and listen.

MEN AND THEIR MODELING

"If, at the end of my life, I haven't transmitted my belief in Christ to my children, then I haven't been faithful to the calling God has given to me."

We caught Gregg, an Omaha real estate developer, at an interesting time. He had just returned from a trip to the East Coast, where he had visited his fourteen-year-old daughter, Beth Ann, who was in her first year at a boarding school in New England.

"I just picked up the pictures from the trip this morning," said Gregg, "and it was all I could do to stop crying. That was the hardest thing I had to do, letting Beth Ann go back East to boarding school. But now that I look back, I have to believe God was in it."

Beth Ann was enrolled in a prep school affiliated with a major church denomination. Early in the academic year, Gregg called the school administration and asked to speak to the person in charge of the spiritual nurturing of the students. The administrator didn't know how to answer. She said no parent had ever asked that question before.

Before Beth Ann left for New England, Gregg took her out for dinner—just the two of them. After a pleasant dinner and warm conversation, Gregg gently asked her, "What do you believe about God?"

"Well, Dad," replied his daughter, "I really believe all that you and Mom have talked about."

That's all Beth Ann would say—or could say. "She wasn't ready to talk about her faith," said Gregg. "So I told her I accepted her as she was, and I reminded her that I loved her unconditionally.

"I can coach my kids on faith, but I can't make them believe what I believe," says Gregg. "You can't argue them into the kingdom. And that's hard for someone like me because I'm used to making things happen."

Making Your Faith Real

David remembers the time when his eight-year-old daughter, Teri, was cleaning the garage. She wasn't getting any cooperation, however, from Jeff, her five-

> "I can coach my kids on faith, but I can't make them believe what I believe."

MEN AND THEIR MODELING

year-old brother. So Teri decided to get her brother in trouble. She told her little brother that Dad wanted to see him.

"In other words, she lied," said David.

When he asked her about it, she didn't want to admit that she made up the story. So David showed her 1 John 1:8–9: "If we claim to be without sin, we deceive ourselves and the truth is not in us. If we confess our sins, he is faithful and just and will forgive us our sins and purify us from all unrighteousness." David lovingly pointed out the need to ask God for forgiveness.

"Teri began crying, but she knew what the right thing was," David said. "It was a hard lesson for her to learn."

Another way to make your faith real, said Fred, is to crack open your Bible when the kids are around. "If they don't see you reading God's Word, then you're not growing. You have to live what you say."

Church attendance can't be helter-skelter, either. "We didn't send our boys to church on Sunday morning, we took them," says Warren. "That's extremely important. It's also not a good witness to drop the kids off at church and drive off, which I've seen happen."

Children are more perceptive than we give them credit for. "Your kids watch you like hawks, and they start watching you awfully early," we heard one father say.

That's right, Dad. When you're home during those most important hours of the day, you're on stage one—front and center. You're the star of the show, and your audience is soaking in everything you say and do.

It's often said that values are *caught* by children, rather than taught. That's why you can't sit down with a thirteen-year-old and say, "Jimmy, we're going to learn a little something about lying today." No, Jimmy learned that lesson a long time ago when he overheard you tell the pastor you were going to be out of town during the church work day (but you never left the city limits that weekend).

One Rhode Island father recalls the time he mentioned to his wife that he was thinking of buying a radar detector for his sports car. Since he was racking up the miles on the freeway, he thought a "fuzzbuster" was just the ticket to outwit the highway patrol.

Leave it to his better half to straighten him out. "Well, what kind of lesson do you want to teach our kids? Do you want to tell them that if you have enough money you can speed and evade the police?" she asked.

Ah, I guess not . . .

It also helps to admit mistakes to your children. If you do mess up, ask your children to forgive you— they do it so easily.

I (Mike) learned that lesson during the summer of 1991, when Focus on the Family moved its Pomona headquarters in Southern California to Colorado Springs. A moving van packed our belongings, and we jumped into the family car for the trip east.

At ten the first night, we pulled into Las Vegas and checked into the Excalibur Hotel, the world's largest with 4,200 rooms. The place is so huge that finding our room was a chore; we entered a wrong door from the parking lot and had to drag our heavy luggage past thousands of slot machines and gaming tables. Tired, cranky, and out of sorts, we thought we'd never find the elevator to our room on the twenty-fourth floor.

The next day at checkout time, I told Nicole I was making a first trip to the car with a couple of bags. I took my seven-year-old son, Patrick, with me. Outside the hotel, the mid-August heat—it was 110 degrees that day—hit us like a sledge hammer. We trudged our way to the far reaches of the parking lot. Wouldn't you know it? When we arrived at the car, I had forgotten the blasted keys.

"Values are caught by children, rather than taught."

MEN AND THEIR MODELING

166

The last thing I wanted to do was lug those bags all the way back to the hotel room, so I asked Patrick if he could "guard" the bags while I ran back to the hotel room for the keys.

I felt a little funny leaving Patrick in the middle of a Las Vegas parking lot, but it was midday. I would only be gone for ten minutes.

When I got back to the room, Nicole asked me where Patrick was. I pointed to the window.

"He's down with the car and luggage," I said.

"What?"

I repeated what I said.

"You stupid jerk!" Nicole screamed.

I bolted back to the elevator, fearing the worst. My only son. Kidnapped. Never to be seen again. When I got to the car, Patrick was standing there, hands in his pockets.

I hugged him, put the bags in the car and walked him back to the hotel room. Then I sat down with him on the queen bed.

"Patrick, Daddy just did a really stupid thing. I left you out with the car all alone, and I shouldn't have done that. I made a big mistake. I'm sorry, and I won't let it happen again. Can you forgive me?"

Patrick cast his eyes downward and whispered, "Sure, Dad. It's okay." I couldn't believe he wasn't mad at me.

I never felt so thankful in my life. Patrick was safe, and I had just experienced the unconditional love of a child. I felt humbled inside.

Some Scenarios

We also have to think through our actions and guard our thoughts. Along these lines, have any of these scenarios crossed your mind before?

- My kids are still asleep when I get up. They'll never see me reading my Bible or praying.

- My son won't comprehend a real relationship with God until he's in his teens. He wouldn't understand what I was trying to say anyway.

- All girls like to read, so my daughter will probably open the Bible without ever needing to see me do it.

- Right now, all the kids want to do is play Super Nintendo. We'll start talking about spiritual things when they hit high school.

- Mealtime prayer is all they can sit still for. Wouldn't they be bored if I started talking about Christ?

No, they wouldn't, not if you talked in your own words and at their level. Realize, too, that Dad sets—or should set—the spiritual temperature around the house. One East Coast father organizes a time of family prayer each month. "We keep a list of prayers in a looseleaf notebook," says Jon, "and every now and then we look back and see how God has answered our prayers. We also go around the table and have everyone write something nice about their brother or sister in the notebook. They might write, 'I like the way Willie shared with me' or 'Julia played real nice with me.' The main idea is that kids remember *something*. Because they have written the nice things down, they can go back and read them anytime and be encouraged."

Ben, a dad from Louisiana, spends ten to fifteen minutes with each child before they go to bed, reviewing their day and praying with them for the next. "I do that to make sure I have time with them each day."

David, from Missoula, Montana, says, "Family devotions may work for some, but I'd rather do Bible studies in the context of life. The Apostle John said 'The Word became flesh and dwelt among us.' Christianity is lived out in the context of relationship, not simply truth. If it were just the truth, Jesus wouldn't

MEN AND THEIR MODELING

have needed to come to earth. He could have just said 'Here boys. Take these words and go get 'em.' I think Moses tried that once. It didn't work so well.

"So now I try to create opportunities where there will be teachable moments. I used to take off and go fishing when I was down, but now I share my struggles and loneliness with my kids. You know what? They minister to me!"

Isn't that great? No fighting to find fifteen minutes in the family schedule. No structured teaching. Just a conviction that Christianity doesn't have to be programmed or forced, but can happen at any hour of the day.

The earlier you start these little rituals—such as genuine communication, a prayer notebook, or devotional time—the more easily they'll be accepted by your children. Any counselor will tell you that values taught early in life have a better chance of sticking. If we put our relationship with God above sports, TV, work, and hobbies, then our children's attitude about loving God will be enhanced. Guaranteed.

Living It Out

Matt has seen lives change since he started praying six mornings a week. "You know how you tell friends who share with you, 'Oh, I'll pray for you,' but you never quite get around to it? Well, I started keeping a prayer diary to keep me on track, and each day, I pray for different topics.

"On Monday it's my work. On Tuesdays it's my church and other Christian organizations. On Wednesdays, my saved and unsaved friends. It's funny, but one unsaved friend from college knows that I pray for him every Wednesday. On Thursdays, I pray for

MEN AND THEIR MODELING

"The earlier you start these little rituals—such as genuine communication, a prayer notebook, or devotional time—the more easily they'll be accepted by your children."

169

my extended family. On Fridays I pray for my spiritual growth. On Saturdays I pray for my own family."

Matt wakes up each morning by 6:00, showers and shaves by 6:20, then spends thirty minutes in prayer and quiet time with the Lord. He doesn't do it out of obligation or mere habit either. He's learned the joy of being a "disciplined disciple." Then he eats breakfast with the kids.

"It's nice to tell people you're praying for them on a regular basis. Since I've started doing this, I've seen lives change. I believe prayer is the nucleus of being a good dad."

Matt has set the high-jump bar of spiritual leadership pretty high. Could you vault it? If a family friend asked your kids what the most important thing in their dad's life was, how would they answer? Better yet, have a friend at church ask the question—if you dare!

They might reply, "*Me!*" or "*Mommy!*" (They'd better not say work!) But are these responses correct? Not according to God, who gave us the right answer in Genesis 22. God asked Abraham to take his only son Isaac and sacrifice him. He was testing Abraham's obedience and value system. Abraham and Sarah had longed eighty years for a son. Isaac was the answer to their prayers. Then God put the ultimate test before Abraham—and he passed. Are you passing yours?

Doing the Small Stuff

Daily or weekly family devotions is one of those ideas that sounds great on paper but is much harder to put into practice. Of the fifty men we interviewed, only a handful said they consistently were able to lead their families in prayer and Bible study.

A typical response came from Kurt. "Trying to be a spiritual leader and establish a regular family devotion time has been difficult," he confessed. "Some-

MEN AND THEIR MODELING

times I become frustrated and lose my patience trying to meet my kids' spiritual needs. It seems as though they're constantly jockeying for my time."

"As for family devotions at home," said another father, "we're finding the shorter, the better. But the consistency is not there for us. I take full blame for that."

Another father said he failed miserably to stick to a regular schedule. "I tried reading C. S. Lewis' *The Narnia Chronicles* when the kids were younger, but it never worked out having devotions each day. I always felt guilty for that."

A pastor we interviewed said he is sensitive about doing anything structured with his kids. "When I was a teenager, I was turned off to God for a long time because I was force-fed the Word. Now that I'm a father, I've tried not to cram things down my own kids' throats. We have no devotional requirements, but my wife and I have sought to model a spiritual discipline to our kids.

"Being a pastor and raising the kids to be spiritually minded is more difficult than it seems. I want them to have a high regard for the Lord, yet I don't want them to feel that my work is more important than they are. Thankfully, they know that *God* is more important, not *God's work*. The result has been that all my kids are ministry-minded. Their hearts have remained tender to the eternal God and the eternal lives of others."

So, what can you do?

Start small. Even sharing a couple of Bible verses at the breakfast table can be a good beginning. Reading a Bible story to the kids as they go down at night will work, too, especially if they get to "stay up" to hear you read. "I've found that the best time to have devotions is when I tuck the kids in bed," said Nick. "Lots of questions pop into their minds, and that's what makes it a magical time. They also talk about things that are bugging them, and when that happens, we talk about what the Word says about it." These types of discussions can lead your children into a deeper relationship with the Lord.

"We also pray together every night," added Louis. "My children are still small, so I pray out loud, and then they pray. I'm even asking the Lord to help us when they grow up to be teenagers and that He will keep us close during that difficult period."

Erik says he tries to pray about big things and little things with his kids. "We've prayed for things that have got lost around the house—stuff I think God isn't concerned about—and it turns out the kids find these toys in a miraculous way. To me, that shows God is more concerned about their spiritual growth than I am."

The capper, says Erik, came when the kids lost an action figure toy at a nearby lake—buried somewhere in the sand. "Even though we had given up hope, we prayed that we would find the toy. When I walked around the lake bed, I had no idea where to look. Then I saw a plastic arm sticking out the sand! That was a good lesson for us. Right there, we learned the reality of prayer for a situation I had no faith for."

While prayer for the child's needs is the glue that will bond his heart to God, unselfish prayer is the super glue. One father makes it a point to pray with his children for unsaved relatives, friends, neighbors—and his child's friends, too. "You can't start too early building God's heart for the lost in your child. It has to be more than prayer—they have to see you in action, too. You begin by talking to God about people—*then* you can talk to people about God. My job isn't complete until my kids love God so much that they can't help but share Him with their friends."

Forget the Guilt

As with most of the topics we've tossed your way, we've left sufficient room for you to get depressed

> *"While prayer for the child's needs is the glue that will bond his heart to God, unselfish prayer is the super glue."*

MEN AND THEIR MODELING

172

about how you're doing. If you've overlooked spiritual modeling in the past, it's not too late to make this a priority. You can start, of course, with *you*. While radical changes may be in order, our counsel is to have a one-step-at-a-time strategy. Don't try to become "Joe Onfire" overnight. Here's a sample strategy to move forward.

Getting Rid of the Past

The Scripture we quoted in 1 John wasn't just a trite verse that applies to kids. It's *the* answer to starting fresh with God. No matter how far away we've walked from Him, all it takes is a quick turnaround, and He's right there with us.

Examining the Present

In a journal, or perhaps just on a piece of paper, take inventory of your walk with God. If you haven't spent any meaningful time with Him for several months, write it down. If you haven't prayed for—or with— your kids in weeks, make a note of that, too. Then resolve to improve.

Setting a Goal

Set a goal for tomorrow. The fastest way to get discouraged is to make lofty goals for sweeping changes. Take a realistic look at your time and ask yourself where you could find five to fifteen minutes to get one-on-one with God. (The best time is before breakfast—before you've settled into the day. Don't think you can pick it up at night. We're too tired.)

Start each quiet time with a prayer like this: "Lord, I don't want to spend time with You because I have to; I want to do this because no one loves me, accepts me, or understands me as You do. I need You.

Guide me and speak loudly to my heart, and make me long for You."

Don't start a detailed prayer list if you've never had one before, and don't give yourself chapter and verse reading requirements. The key is getting thirsty for God again. If you drown yourself in major changes, the changes *will not last.*

Choosing Friends

Tell your wife, a friend at church, even your pastor, that you're trying to make some big changes through some small steps. Tell them you would covet their prayers. No real friend would turn down that invitation for help.

Finally . . .

Realizing That Your Schedule
Will Probably Not Be "God Friendly"

Satan works against us by keeping us away from things that will benefit us the most. His patient strategy is to keep us off balance and too busy to muster much spiritual hunger for God. He's successfully torpedoed generations, convincing them to reject—or neglect—Christ as their leader and authority. Most of the time we don't even realize Satan's been at work until it's too late.

We had fathers tell us that Satan's goal is to get us so entrenched in everyday life that we would be too discouraged even to think about digging out of the abyss. Once we've lost the motivation to keep plugging along, he's succeeded. Many men will throw up their hands and complain that there's no hope.

If we can leave you one thought from this book, it's this:

There is always hope! No rut is too deep, no trench is too wide, no schedule is too hectic, and no heart is

MEN AND THEIR MODELING

too cold for God. He will graciously allow you to start all over.

God is a miracle worker who delights in shedding light into the darkness of "hopeless" situations—like us. If your heart truly desires change, pray diligently. Don't give up until you're where you want to be. Then, by the Lord's mercy, you'll take one step toward Him . . . and another.

Man to Man

1. Identify important ways in which your spiritual journey provides role modeling for your children. In what ways would you like to improve the role modeling?

2. In what ways might your children signal their readiness for spiritual decision making or for understanding the ethical issues they will face for the rest of their lives?

3. Work out a reasonable plan for enchancing your connection with God through study, prayer, and sharing with others. Remember not to try to do too much at once.

"There is always hope! No rut is too deep, no trench is too wide, no schedule is too hectic, and no heart is too cold for God."

MEN AND THEIR MODELING

15

GETTING PERSONAL

Men and Their "Spare Time"

*H*ave we forgotten anything? Let's see, so far we've covered:

- cutting back on work if it's affecting your family time
- how to spend more time with your kids
- building your wife's self-esteem
- helping out by doing more things around the house
- spending more time with God through prayer and Bible study
- using your spiritual gifts
- sharing your faith with neighbors and co-workers
- keeping your mind clean
- and having close friendships with other men

If the ax is dull and its edge unsharpened, more strength is needed but skill will bring success.
Ecclesiastes

That's quite a list. Just reviewing it is enough to wear out any weary dad.

Oh, yes, one last thing: how about personal time for you? (You have our permission to laugh and ask "What's that?")

Among us fathers, we can agree that "time for ourselves" is a pretty hilarious topic. We're always last in line . . . but that's okay. It's like being captain of a passenger ship; you're always the last to leave a sinking liner. It comes with the territory.

At a men's retreat, we conducted a survey that asked the fathers what activities they would drop if life got too hectic. The top three were

1. reading the newspaper

2. exercise

3. hobbies

While we accept those responses, we also know men aren't happy campers when they have little time to goof off. When life gets too busy (and when kids enter the picture, it usually does), we're left with three choices:

1. Play the martyr and pretend we don't really need time for ourselves.

2. Say "heck with this" and go do our own thing, no matter how it affects the family.

3. Find ways to include much-needed personal time in our over-scheduled lives.

The best alternative, of course, is the third one. While more men find themselves playing the martyr or doing their own thing, both have negative long-term results.

Getting Your Space

Perhaps you spent nine or ten hours at the office today, plus another forty-five minutes fighting traffic, heat, and smog. As you ease your sedan into the driveway, the kids come running out. They've been waiting three hours for you to get home to play with them, and they're wired to blow. What do you do?

MEN AND THEIR "SPARE TIME"

That's what has happened to me (Greg) for the last couple of years. I love it, I really do . . . okay, most of the time. But other dads may work in a more stressful environment than Focus on the Family—they need some time to air out.

If we play the martyr, we shouldn't expect the family to read our minds. And when nobody notices the sacrifices we make, we'll slip into a bad mood, thinking no one appreciates anything we do. (Women are right. Men *are* babies sometimes.)

When Marty arrives home, his wife tries to sense what type of day he's had at the office. "She acts as a buffer between me and the kids," he says. "After our twins were born, we put this into practice. It gives me time to collect my thoughts and get ready to be a constructive part of the family."

Another father, Skip, said, "Sometimes you go home, and all you want to do is sit down, kick up your feet, and read a newspaper. I try not to do that. I listen to my six-year-old babble on for fifteen minutes. She can talk the arms off a brass monkey."

Other men told us they have a ten-minute timeout rule after they walk in the front door. Dad's given a few minutes to change his clothes, check the mail, and talk to Mom before it's open season for the kids.

That's a good idea—as long as you don't make it a ten-hour rule. But several fathers said the key was showing some flexibility so the wife and kids don't get their feelings hurt by a stressed-out grump.

MEN AND THEIR "SPARE TIME"

"Women are right. Men are babies sometimes."

Doing What You Love

For me (Greg), the ideal "Honey-I'm-home" routine is to kiss my wife, say hi to the boys, get out of my suit and tie, scan the mail, turn on the nightly news and read the paper—thirty minutes to do what I want. Real personal time! This happens about once every six months—and only on the days Elaine and the kids aren't home!

Who wouldn't love an hour of racquetball before dinner, or a chance to tinker in the garage or curl up with a new Tom Clancy novel? Perhaps you can pull it off, but the rest of us mortals have to strong-arm our schedules to pick up a free hour here and there. When we asked our fathers how many hours a week they read for pleasure, the results were

- none—1 percent
- one to two hours—37 percent
- three to five hours—50 percent
- six to ten hours—12 percent

These figures were higher than the number of hours our fathers said they watch TV each week. In other words, they read more than they watch TV, which is an encouraging development.

The best—and usually only—time to read is after the kids are in bed. Leave the TV off. Reading also promotes communication with your wife. I (Mike) always find it easier to put my book down when Nicole talks to me (since I can come right back to my place) than to turn my eyes away from the TV set.

Another way I've won back time has been to take advantage of Focus on the Family's flextime policy. I start work at 7:30 A.M., which means I'm pulling into my driveway a few minutes before five o'clock. That gives me enough time to go on a bike ride with the kids, hit tennis balls with them, or see one of Patrick's soccer games.

When I moved to Los Angeles to join Dr. Dobson's ministry, we settled in a neighborhood about eight blocks from the main headquarters. I could walk to my office—which I did a couple of times. Living close to work goes against the grain of most Southern Californians, who wear their two-hour commutes like a red badge of courage.

MEN AND THEIR "SPARE TIME"

Well, I didn't want a stinking badge. And you know what? I actually *liked* Los Angeles during my five years there. I always told my friends, "If you can beat the freeways, L.A. is a lot better place to live." And when Focus on the Family moved twenty miles from Arcadia to Pomona, I moved eastward, too. (Fortunately, we were renting and the kids weren't in school yet, so it was an easy move.)

Speaking of commutes, the fathers we surveyed seemed to have that under control. The morning commute averaged fifteen minutes; the evening drive was a bit longer: 16.7 minutes.

Anyway, Nicole and I settled near a great tennis club because we love to play. Tennis is my sport and my hobby, and I enjoy teaching Andrea and Patrick how to hit forehands and backhands.

We talked to men whose hobbies can be shared with their kids, too. Here are a few examples:

- stamp collecting
- gardening
- woodworking
- collecting sports cards
- setting up electric train sets
- computer games
- reading
- working on the car
- sports the entire family can do (basketball shooting, skiing, ice skating, softball, etc.)
- attending ballgames as a family instead of with the guys.

Some claim the best hobby of all is watching sports on TV. That doesn't count, Dad. While sharing a seventh game of a World Series or a Super Bowl matchup certainly qualifies as family time, letting an ESPN college basketball triple header drone on and on is not.

MEN AND THEIR "SPARE TIME"

"The best—and usually only—time to read is after the kids are in bed. Leave the TV off. Reading also promotes communication with your wife."

"My obsession is sports," confessed Guy. "It's easy to get glued to the tube. Though it's not a day-in and day-out problem, watching sports bothers my wife because I tune out the family."

Choose your viewing wisely. You can't follow every sport, every league, every game. Pro and college sports are all over the tube, and there's a game on every night. You'll live if you don't see every touchdown or every home run.

Here's what I (Mike) do if there's a great game or tennis tournament on during a beautiful Sunday afternoon: I tape the event on my VCR. Then, a few hours later, I rewind the tape and fast-forward through the event. NBA basketball games are a joke. Nothing happens until the fourth quarter when the players turn up the intensity level. Then it takes half an hour to play the final two minutes. With a VCR, I can zip my way through all the timeouts and zillions of commercials. I can watch a Celtics game in twenty minutes, and with tennis matches, I can fast-forward to four-all in each set.

The only drawback to taping sports happens when I run into a friend before I've seen the event. "Did you see that half-court shot Larry Bird swished to beat the Lakers?" my buddy exclaims.

"No, I didn't," I reply through clenched teeth. "I was planning on watching the game later."

At times like that, I resist the urge to deck my close friend.

Fitting in the "E" Word

For some men, exercise is an obsession. For others, exercise was something they did in gym class twenty years and fifty pounds ago. This topic needs a Top Ten list. Here's our last one.

MEN AND THEIR "SPARE TIME"

182

The Top Ten Reasons
Not to Join a Health Club

10 On your first no-cost visit to Biff's Body Bar, you were caught leaving the club with a twenty-five-pound barbell in your gym bag because you didn't know what "free-weight" meant.

9 To pay someone just so you can exercise is definitely not good stewardship.

8 Locker-room talk with a bunch of overweight men isn't half as interesting as it was in high school.

7 Like most health club members, you'd probably work out only five or six times a year, so why not just skip it and pocket the cash?

6 If you join a health club, you'll discover just how out of shape you really are (talk about depressing).

5 People will see your legs.

4 If you try pumping iron with the big boys, you'll only bruise your ego . . . and pull every muscle in your body!

3 You don't have the right shoes, and your wife would never let you take out a loan to buy a pair.

2 The girls in the skimpy aerobics outfits could be hazardous to your health—if your wife ever caught you looking at them.

1 You're too old to be healthy.

Okay, now that you're convinced you shouldn't join a health club, you're off the hook, right?

MEN AND THEIR "SPARE TIME"

Well, we don't think so. We believe exercise is a great way to relieve stress and keep the old waistline from expanding. It can also be a great family activity. But 18 percent of the men we surveyed said they don't exercise at all. They also said they don't miss it (and we believed them!). Fine. You don't *have* to keep the body toned up.

But some of us prefer working out and staying in shape. We like the good feeling that goes along with it. We enjoy the competition and the challenge of pushing our bodies to the limit. If you're one of those folks, you should consider joining a health club of some sort (fitness, tennis, or golf). In case you're wondering, 33 percent of the surveyed fathers said they belong to a club.

Here are a few tips on health clubs:

- *Pick one close to home.* If you have to drive twenty minutes or more one-way to exercise, the time cost will be too high.

- *Purchase a family membership.* That way, you can take the kids, too. Many clubs have a children's play area which they can use while you make the rounds of the Nautilus machines.

- *Make sure the club has a swimming pool.* Children love to swim, and there's nothing better than having the whole family around the pool on a hot summer's day. In Southern California, we (Mike and Nicole) used to pack a picnic dinner and go for a twilight swim with the kids—a great way to cool them off.

- *Ask other members if the club is "kid friendly."* Some clubs are havens for the social set who believe kids should be seen and not heard. You want to join a club where kids are welcome.

- *Finally, if a club is beyond your budget, use municipal facilities.* Many towns and cities have a public pool and parks with fantastic facilities. Use them—after all, you're paying for their upkeep, too!

"Exercise is a great way to relieve stress and keep the old waistline from expanding. It can also be a great family activity."

MEN AND THEIR "SPARE TIME"

Staying in Shape at Work

Once you've resolved to get in better shape, the dilemma (as usual) is finding time to exercise without leaving the family in the dust.

Most of the men we talked to incorporated exercise into their daily routine. Here are several examples: *At work* . . .

- If your office building has a shower, go jogging or run the stairs at noon. Eat a light lunch afterward.
- If you can't change out of your work clothes, bring soft shoes and go for a brisk walk.
- Play tennis, basketball, or racquetball before work.
- Take stairs instead of elevators. Climbing steps is a great aerobic activity.
- Keep moving during the work day. Don't be desk bound.

With the family . . .

- Biking. Many towns have constructed bike paths. Be sure to wear helmets.
- Hiking. We're not talking about shinnying up a sheer cliff. No, we're talking about going for a walk in the woods or a scenic spot near town.
- Although we've mentioned this in other places, shoot baskets, flip the Frisbee, hit tennis balls, or play catch with the kids.
- Take on outdoor projects, such as yard work or big chores around the house. Mowing grass and hauling tree limbs will increase your heart rate, too.
- Pop an exercise video in the VCR and do aerobics together. The kids will be entertained, and you and your spouse will get a workout.

It's hard to keep the big picture in mind when you exercise. But remember this: By exercising now, you increase your chances of being around when the grandkids arrive and grow up. By eating right and staying in shape (especially if you're a desk jockey with a silk rope and a leather lunch bucket), you should be around to influence two generations of your family.

My dad (Greg) grew up in the era when adults smoked and drank. He never paid much attention to his health, and it showed. He died at age fifty-five from heart disease. Sadly, his grandkids never got a chance to know him very well.

Who knows? The time you spend with your children's children could make the difference whether they come to know Christ.

"By exercising now, you increase your chances of being around when the grandkids arrive and grow up."

Man to Man

1. Write down a general assessment of your present personal time? How much do you have? When do you have it?

2. What needs do you satisfy when you use your personal time?

3. Can you think of ways to make personal use of other time—driving, taking the kids to their appointments, working around the house, etc.?

MEN AND THEIR "SPARE TIME"

16

BACK TO THE FUTURE

Men and Regret

I slipped in the key, turned the lock, and stepped into my dark living room.

"Surprise!"

The cheers nearly bowled me over. As the lights flipped on, I saw black balloons and crepe paper hanging from every corner. "Way to go, Greg, you're a half-century old now," yelled one of my buddies.

It was July 11, 2006. My fiftieth birthday! Yuk!

My best friends were out in force, arriving with presents fit for someone ready to be carted off to a rest home. The "gifts" merely twisted the knife: Dentu-grip, adult diapers, Geritol, two hot-water bottles, "The Best of Lawrence Welk" (in dual-sided videodisc!), and a lifetime subscription to *Modern Maturity*. I took the gifts in stride, and I enjoyed every embarrassing moment.

But it wasn't *just* my fiftieth birthday. It was also the day after my thirtieth wedding anniversary to the bride of my youth, Elaine.

And today was also a huge day for my youngest son, Drew, whose birthday is also July 11. He was celebrating a milestone of his own, his twenty-first birthday. After

Well done, good and faithful servant! You have been faithful with a few things; I will put you in charge of many things. Come and share your master's happiness!

Matthew

187

one more year of college, he says he's ready to tackle the world. (Or will it be the other way around?)

For twenty-one years on July 11, the spotlight has always shone a little brighter on Drew, which was always fine with me. But fifty simply couldn't be brushed aside. It was my day, and even Drew didn't mind taking a back seat for a change. (He knew he'd get it back next year!)

After all the guests had said their goodbyes, Drew approached me.

"Well, Pop, you're fifty," he said, giving me a light punch on the shoulder. "Good job, you old geezer. Now when are you going to let me beat you on the golf course?"

"Not this year," I grinned.

"I don't know about that. You've been going downhill for a long time."

"Not as quick as you'd like though."

Drew paused, then looked around to see if anyone could hear him.

"Really, Dad, I wanted to ask you kind of a serious question."

"I haven't been serious all night," I laughed, "so why should I start now. But if you want to, ask away."

"Is there anything over the last fifty years that you really regret? If you had it to do over again, would you have done anything differently?"

Whoa! Rewind the tape fourteen years—

Back to the Present

I'm not fifty! Whew! But I *am* thirty-six. I'm not quite ready for the Geritol crowd, but I'm certainly prepared to reflect on where my life is right now . . . and where I want to be fourteen years from now when the fateful fiftieth hits.

MEN AND REGRET

Thirty-six is a good spot to be in. I'm old enough to learn from the mistakes I've made, but young enough to still make some fine-tuning changes.

Like most people, however, I carry some baggage from thirty-six years of life on this earth (eighteen of them without Christ). Though God's given me a lovely wife and two of the greatest boys around, I wish I could have changed some things: hurting responses I've made; actions I had to seek forgiveness for; and missed opportunities to share my faith with family and neighbors. And I still battle some bigger issues daily:

- allowing the newspaper to come before my time with God too often

- watching too much sports on TV (cable sports addictions will be the next wave of Treatment Center ads.)

- not romancing Elaine as often as I used to (The excuse of no time or no money always *seemed* so valid, but what better way could I show my boys how to be a diligent husband who loves his wife?)

- not praying enough with Elaine during the good times (It was easy to be on our knees when tough times hit—like when Troy had three major surgeries to repair a birth defect or when Dad died a few years ago. But God was left out of too many days and weeks when there wasn't a crisis. I wonder how He feels about that?)

- not praying enough *with* and *for* my boys

Taken too far, these and other regrets could be unhealthy—especially if you're like me, too introspective. I could easily wallow in all of the things I didn't do and could feel *very* guilty. Depression could then handcuff my motivation to change.

The Apostle Paul told the Philippians, "But one thing I do: Forgetting what is behind and straining toward what is ahead, I press on toward the goal to

MEN AND REGRET

"Regrets could be unhealthy . . . I could easily wallow in all of the things I didn't do and could feel very guilty."

win the prize for which God has called me heaven-ward in Christ Jesus" (3:13–14).

Forgetting the past—and also learning from it—is what Paul was good at.

Planning for the Future

That's why I'm trying today to grab hold of what I want my life to be like in the future. I don't want to hit fifty and have a long list of regrets for what I could have done, especially concerning my family.

I made a list of some things I *don't* want to say to Drew if he asks me that question fourteen years from now:

- *"I'm sorry I was gone so much while you and Troy were growing up."* Now's the time to get in-volved in their world through coaching, Sunday school, or scouting. I want them to think it's normal to have Dad around a lot. Maybe then they'll be diligent dads themselves.

- *"Your mother and I love each other, but we have our own interests now."* I don't want to wake up the day after my youngest moves out, dreading the next thirty years. I suppose some things are worse than not being best friends with your wife, but I don't know what they would be.

- *"I tried to get you kids to church and model godly disciplines, but we were a busy family."* What a tragedy it would be if I didn't pass a diligent and loving relationship with Jesus Christ on to my sons. In a world with few standards and too many wrong choices, my boys are going to need a solid Christian foundation to make correct de-cisions. If it's not the Bible, it will be something that's second best—or worse!

MEN AND REGRET

190

Fourteen years from now, there will be some things that I know I'll regret. I won't be able to rid myself completely of the consequences of my sin nature.

But I want that list to be a short one, so if Drew sits down with me that night of my fiftieth birthday (or any night!), I can tell him, "Son, I made it my goal to live a life I would never regret. I've failed in some areas, as you know. But I made a choice to learn from my past and look forward to the future.

"More than anything else, Son, I want to hear Jesus say, '*Well done good and faithful servant. . . .*' "

MEN AND REGRET

Man to Man

1. Imagine your own fiftieth (sixtieth, seventieth) birthday. Given your present lifestyle, what might you regret?

2. What things are you doing today that will help you face that birthday in the not-so-distant future?

3. What are you doing today to pass a disciplined and loving relationship with Christ along to your children?

"More than anything else, Son, I want to hear Jesus say, 'Well done, good and faithful servant.' "

EPILOGUE
A Battle Plan

*P*erhaps you're asking yourself the question: "So, what do I do now?"

As we said at the outset, don't try to take on too much, or you'll only get frustrated and give up trying to change anything. Instead, grab a pencil and look at the list below.

First, put a star next to the statements that aren't really true or don't need your immediate attention.

❏ My job is asking too much of me and of my family.

❏ My earthly father was a poor example, and I believe it has affected my performance as a dad and husband.

❏ My kids aren't getting enough of my time to insure they'll be on my team when they're older.

❏ I don't often communicate to my wife how special she really is.

❏ I'm not *properly* romancing my wife.

❏ Our sex life can use an overhaul.

❏ My thought life needs more capturing and less surrendering.

❏ Closer friendships with other men should be pursued.

❏ I'm serving too much in the church.

❏ I'm not giving God and the church enough of my time.

❏ I need to be doing more to share my faith with (choose those that apply) friends, co-workers, neighbors, or relatives.

❏ I don't have a good perspective on spending time with God, and I'm not motivated to be with Him on a consistent basis.

❏ I need to be a better spiritual example to my children.

❏ I need to put a little of myself back into my schedule, either through exercise or hobbies.

See, you're not such a bad guy after all!

Now, rank the ones you didn't star in the order of what will benefit you most the next ten years. If you want to be really brave, ask your wife to give her opinion on a separate sheet of paper. You don't have to show her what you chose, but if they don't match up fairly closely, you may want to do some more evaluating.

Finally, take your top two responses and write down a brief battle plan in the space provided below. Feel free to use any of the practical ideas we've mentioned.

Area Number One _____

1. I need to change these attitudes if I'm going to get better:

A BATTLE PLAN

2. I need to do these things:

3. I will ask this person to hold me accountable to this goal:

Area Number Two _____

1. I need to change these attitudes if I'm going to get better:

2. I need to do these things:

3. I will ask this person to hold me accountable to this goal:

*Good luck, God bless,
And thanks for joining us!*

APPENDIX ONE

Survey Results For "Daddy's Home"

*H*ere are the complete results of our survey (no, Price and Waterhouse didn't audit these figures, but they've been checked several times by us).

Average age: 42.5 years

A. Marriage

1. Are you married, remarried, or widowed?
   - 95 percent were married
   - 4 percent were remarried
   - 1 percent were widowed

2. How long have you been married?
   - 18.6 years

3. Please list your children and their ages.
   - Our fathers had an average of 2.65 kids.

4. How long did you court your wife before you became engaged?
   - less than three months—11 percent
   - 3–6 months—12 percent
   - 6–9 months—2 percent
   - 9–12 months—20 percent
   - 1–2 years—21 percent
   - more than 2 years—34 percent

5. How long was your engagement?
   - less than three months—12 percent
   - 3–6 months—30 percent
   - 6–9 months—23 percent

- 9–12 months—22 percent
- 1–2 years—11 percent
- more than 2 years—2 percent

6. Have you adopted any children?

- yes—6 percent
- no—94 percent

7. How often do you visit your *wife's* side of the family?

- We see her family and relatives a lot (every week)—18 percent.
- We see them occasionally (once every 2–3 weeks)—16 percent.
- We see them once a month—17 percent.
- We see them just during the holidays—24 percent.
- We seldom see them—25 percent.

8. How often do you visit *your* side of the family?

- We see my family and relatives a lot (every week)—15 percent.
- We see them occasionally (once every 2–3 weeks)—19 percent.
- We see them once a month—19 percent.
- We see them just during the holidays—19 percent.
- We seldom see them—28 percent.

B. Home and Work

1. Do you own your own home?

- yes—97 percent
- no—3 percent

2. How long is your morning commute?

- 15 minutes

3. How long is your evening commute?

- 16.7 minutes

SURVEY RESULTS FOR "DADDY'S HOME"

4. What time do you leave in the morning?
   - 7:15

5. Return home at night?
   - 5:40

6. Do you take public transportation?
   - yes—3 percent
   - no—95 percent
   - occasionally—2 percent

7. How many cars does your family own?
   - 2.49 cars

8. How many hours do you work each day?
   - 9.3 hours

9. How many days do you work each week?
   - 5.1 days

10. Are you paid extra for overtime?
    - yes—8 percent
    - no—92 percent

11. How much overtime do you work each week?
    - 11.2 hours

12. Do you ever bring work home?
    - yes—71 percent
    - no—29 percent

13. If so, how many hours a week do you work at home at night?
    - weeknights—3.5 hours
    - weekends—1.8 hours

14. Does your wife work outside the home?
    - yes—33 percent
    - no—67 percent

15. If so, how many hours a week?
    - 24 hours

SURVEY RESULTS FOR "DADDY'S HOME"

16. Does your wife have a home-based business?
    - yes—9 percent
    - no—91 percent

C. Personal

1. How many times a week do you exercise or participate in sports?
   - none—18 percent
   - once a week—15 percent
   - 2–3 times a week—30 percent
   - 3–4 times a week—19 percent
   - 5–7 times a week—18 percent

2. What sports do you participate in?
   - Running, golf, tennis, basketball, softball, and skiing were most mentioned.

3. Do you belong to a health, golf, or tennis club?
   - yes—33 percent
   - no—67 percent

4. How fulfilled do you feel about your work?
   - very fulfilled—39 percent
   - fulfilled—44 percent
   - not so fulfilled—14 percent
   - unfulfilled—3 percent

5. How important is feeling fulfilled about work?
   - very important—39 percent
   - important—57 percent
   - not very important—3 percent
   - not important at all—1 percent

6. Do you belong to any civic organizations (Rotary, Lions, etc.)?
   - yes—25 percent
   - no—75 percent

SURVEY RESULTS FOR "DADDY'S HOME"

7. Do you volunteer your time at your local church?
   - yes—87 percent
   - no—13 percent

8. Have you been a volunteer coach?
   - yes—50 percent
   - no—50 percent

9. How much time do you spend with close friends outside of work?
   - no time—14 percent
   - an hour or so a week—36 percent
   - several hours a week—50 percent
   - a couple of days a week—0 percent

10. How many hours a week do you read for pleasure?
    - none—1 percent
    - 1–2 hours—37 percent
    - 3–5 hours—50 percent
    - 6–10 hours—12 percent

11. How many vacation days have you taken in the last year?
    - none—4 percent
    - 1–4 days—3 percent
    - one week—5 percent
    - between one and two weeks—6 percent
    - two weeks—19 percent
    - two to three weeks—25 percent
    - three weeks—12 percent
    - more than three weeks—26 percent

12. How much TV do you watch each day?

    On Weeknights?
    - none—29 percent
    - 1–2 hours—61 percent
    - 2–4 hours—9 percent

SURVEY RESULTS FOR "DADDY'S HOME"

- 4–6 hours—1 percent
- more than 6 hours—0 percent

On Weekends

- none—13 percent
- 1–2 hours—54 percent
- 2–4 hours—28 percent
- 4–6 hours—5 percent
- more than 6 hours—0 percent

13. Do you drink alcohol?
    - yes—34 percent
    - no—66 percent

    If so, how much?

    - several times a week—30 percent
    - once a week—23 percent
    - once a month—17 percent
    - once every few months—30 percent

D. Courting Your Wife

1. Which statement best describes your marital situation?
   - My wife and I are so busy—or our finances are so tight—that it's rare that we're able to go out alone or with friends for an evening—13 percent.
   - We try to go out to dinner or a movie as often as we can, but it's only once a month—38 percent.
   - I try to take my wife out at least once a week—46 percent.
   - Other—3 percent.

2. How would you describe your sex life?
   - I'm very happy and satisfied—51 percent.
   - It's adequate—18 percent.
   - Sometimes it's good, sometimes it's not—15 percent.

SURVEY RESULTS FOR "DADDY'S HOME"

- It could be better—15 percent.
- Nonexistent—1 percent.

E. Spiritual

1. How long have you been a Christian?
   - 22.9 years

2. Were you a Christian before you married?
   - yes—71 percent
   - no—29 percent

3. Was your wife a Christian before you were married?
   - yes—77 percent
   - no—23 percent

4. How often do you attend church?
   - not very often—0 percent
   - once a month—0 percent
   - several times a month—12 percent
   - every Sunday—63 percent
   - every Sunday plus one weeknight service—25 percent

5. Are you involved in a small Bible study group each week?
   - yes—51 percent
   - no—49 percent

6. Are you involved with a men's group for accountability and encouragement?
   - yes—45 percent
   - no—55 percent

7. How often do you read your Bible?
   - not at all—2 percent
   - once a month—6 percent
   - once a week—8 percent
   - several times a week—47 percent
   - daily—37 percent

8. Are you satisfied with this amount?
   - yes—23 percent
   - no—55 percent
   - sometimes—22 percent

9. Do you talk about your Christian faith with:
   - neighbors—48 percent
   - relatives—80 percent
   - co-workers—91 percent
   - strangers—40 percent

10. How many Christian-based books have you read in the last year?
   - none—5 percent
   - 1–2—28 percent
   - 3–5—36 percent
   - more than 5—31 percent

11. Do you give money to your local church?
   - yes—99 percent
   - no—1 percent

12. If so, what percent of your annual income?
   - less than 1 percent—2 percent
   - 1–2 percent—7 percent
   - 3–5 percent—11 percent
   - 5–7 percent—22 percent
   - 7–10 percent—33 percent
   - more than 10 percent—25 percent

13. Do you financially support other Christian organizations?
   - yes—97 percent
   - no—3 percent

14. If so, with what percent of your annual income?
   - less than 1 percent—15 percent
   - 1–2 percent—20 percent

- 3–5 percent—24 percent
- 5–7 percent—26 percent
- 7–10 percent—10 percent
- more than 10 percent—15 percent

SURVEY RESULTS FOR "DADDY'S HOME"

APPENDIX TWO
What Makes A Good Dad?

*H*ere's a list of attributes fathers said were essential characteristics of a good dad. We looked at this list and immediately realized no one could measure up to all of them. But it gave the two of us some ideas about a few qualities we need to work on ourselves. Try to do the same.

- Someone who's a good role model as a husband, father, friend, worker, volunteer, and church member, but above all as a Christian.
- Someone who loves enough to listen.
- Someone who instructs—but not like a tyrant.
- Someone who is willing to get off the wall and crazy with his kids on occasion.
- Someone who can admit his mistakes.
- Someone who, if he says no to his children, offers fun alternatives.
- Someone who's consistent in his moral life.
- Someone who creates teachable moments.
- Someone who, when the children are older, has the ability to negotiate with them and try to set up win-win situations.
- Someone who models spiritual disciplines, but doesn't try to cram them down another's throat.
- Someone who tries to be a good husband first. (Since the mom meets many of the needs of the kids, the husband has to meet the needs of the wife.)
- Someone who doesn't judge his kids based on performance.

WHAT MAKES A GOOD DAD?

- Someone who knows the proper balance between love and discipline for each child.

- Someone who, when he blows it, is the first one to say so.

- Someone who grows with his children instead of just watching them grow.

- Someone who never belittles his kids' dreams.

- Someone who doesn't stop pursuing quality family time just because the kids are older and busier.

- Someone who leads by example, rather than bellowing out orders.

- Someone who talks to, and not at, his child.

- Someone who is involved in his children's lives without pulling the reins so tight that they have no room to make decisions—and mistakes—on their own.

- Someone who's strong enough to face squarely the tough issues of life and not fear them (specifically, his own sexuality and his relationship with his dad).

- Someone who's content with his strengths and weaknesses, but seeks to continually improve himself to serve God and his family better.

- Someone who knows how to "major on the majors" and "minor on the minors."

- Someone who knows the negative influences his child faces and seeks to deal with them appropriately.

- Someone who provides financially without becoming addicted to the work and its ego-building entrapments.

- Someone who leads his family in reaching out to others.

- Someone who pursues his kids, not waiting for them to make the first move.

- Someone who loves them in the way their heavenly Father would love them.

- Someone who's "engaged" by being willing to be totally involved with his children and enter into their world with full energy and attention (as much as, or more than, he engages in his favorite hobby).

- Someone who allows God to be in control (Lord) of his life. (Then, most of the rest will fall into place.)

- Someone who identifies with his kids' emotional experiences (when they're hurt by a friend, lose an animal friend, or face the hard lessons on love and the opposite sex).

- Someone who disciplines appropriately, but also compliments, rewards, and reinforces good behavior and character qualities even more often.

- Someone who gives his children a sense of mission, the idea that the Lord has a special task for each of them.

- Someone who willingly and openly discusses whatever the children want to discuss, regardless of the topic.

- Someone who realizes that a man's children get their ideas of who God is by observing their dad.

- Someone who lets his children see him fail and recover in a godly manner.

- Someone who strives to have all the answers, but readily admits he doesn't, as he directs his family to seek God's assistance in everything.

WHAT MAKES A GOOD DAD?

APPENDIX THREE
What Makes A Good Husband?

- Someone who is a good friend.
- Someone who spends as much time talking to her as he possibly can.
- Someone who is faithful.
- Someone who gives his wife attention, who listens, interacts, and shows her he cares about her and what she says and does.
- Someone who shows her he values her by helping out with the kids.
- Someone who concentrates on each other's strengths and not their individual differences.
- Someone who always listens, comforts, loves, cherishes, and protects his wife.
- Someone who expresses his love for her by giving her freedom.
- Someone who constantly wins the battle with selfishness.
- Someone who lets the kids know he loves and is committed to his wife.
- Someone willing to change and bend.
- Someone who shares experiences in life with her and also is interested in her life, pursuits, and interests.
- Someone who strives to know what makes his wife tick.
- Someone who doesn't criticize his wife with attempts at humor.
- Someone who rewards and reinforces his wife when she does things he appreciates.

- Someone who tells his wife he loves her on the spur of the moment—for the sole reason that he loves her.

- Someone who prays with and for her that she grows in her relationship with the Lord.

- Someone who's willing to be the spiritual leader of the home, being the kind of husband who wins the respect of his wife so that she willingly follows him.

- Someone who communicates in words and deeds that Christ is number one in his life.

WHAT MAKES A GOOD HUSBAND?

SUBJECT INDEX

213

"DADDY'S HOME"

___ ABOUT THE AUTHORS

*G*REG JOHNSON is the editor of *Breakaway*, a magazine for boys. Prior to joining Focus on the Family in 1989, Greg worked ten years with Youth for Christ in Eugene, Oregon, and Seattle, Washington. Married fifteen years to his wife, Elaine, they are parents of two boys, Troy and Drew. Greg is also the author of *If I Could Ask God One Question* (Tyndale) and co-author of *Getting Ready for the Guy/Girl Thing* (Regal).

MIKE YORKEY is a former newspaper editor who became editor of *Focus on the Family* magazine in 1986. He married Nicole in 1979, and they have two children, Andrea and Patrick. Mike was general editor of *Growing a Healthy Home* (Wolgemuth & Hyatt), a compilation of articles from *Focus on the Family* magazine.

Both authors live in Colorado Springs, Colorado.